A CLOSER LOOK

AT EMANCIPATION 1848

KATHLEEN D. DOWLING

AuthorHouse™
1663 Liberty Drive
Bloomington, IN 47403
www.authorhouse.com
Phone: 833-262-8899

Because of the dynamic nature of the Internet, any web addresses or links contained in this book may have changed
since publication and may no longer be valid. The views expressed in this work are solely those of the author and do
not necessarily reflect the views of the publisher, and the publisher hereby disclaims any responsibility for them.

Any people depicted in stock imagery provided by Getty Images are models,
and such images are being used for illustrative purposes only.
Certain stock imagery © Getty Images.

This book is printed on acid-free paper.

ISBN: 979-8-8230-2532-4 (sc)
ISBN: 979-8-8230-2533-1 (e)

Library of Congress Control Number: 2024907832

Print information available on the last page.

Published by AuthorHouse 05/07/2024

authorHOUSE®

DEDICATION

THIS BOOK IS DEDICATED TO MARIO C. MOORHEAD, IN APPRECIATION OF YOUR MANY YEARS OF *"IN-FOR-MAAAA-TION 'ANNNNNNND' ENLIGHTENMENT IN THE COMPANY OF [Y]OUR DISCOURSE……"* BELOVED, WE SINCERELY THANK YOU!!!

"FREEDOM IS NOT SOMETHING THAT ONE PEOPLE CAN BESTOW ON ANOTHER AS A GIFT. THEY CLAIM IT AS THEIR OWN AND NONE CAN KEEP IT FROM THEM."

~~~

KWAME NKRUMAH
(1909 – 1972)

"INTELLECTUALS OUGHT TO STUDY THE PAST, NOT FOR THE PLEASURE THEY FIND IN SO DOING, BUT TO DERIVE LESSONS FROM IT."

~~~

CHEIKH ANTA DIOP
(1923 - 1986)

CONTENTS

Chapter I: FREDERIKS FORT EXAMINATIONS...1

         A: The Honorable John Gottlieb (aka "General Buddhoe") 2

         B: Major Jacob Heitmann Gyllich (aka "Major Gyllich") 3

         C: The Honorable Martin King (aka "Admiral Martin King")...............4

Chapter II: CHRISTIANSVAERN FORT EXAMINATIONS...................................15

         A: Fort Commander Anton Ulrich Troels Vinzel Falbe.......................16

         B: First Lieutenant Arnold Johan von Meincke.................................19

         C: Royal Councillor Bernhard von Petersen 25

Chapter III: OTHER DEPOSITIONS 27

Chapter IV: EYEWITNESS NARRATIVES.. 38

Chapter V: GENERAL BUDDHOE'S FAMILY 62

Chapter VI: ADMIRAL MARTIN KING'S FAMILY 73

Chapter VII: BUDDHOE'S EMANCIPATION DAY ACTIVITIES 84

Chapter VIII: MARTIN KING'S EMANCIPATION DAY ACTIVITIES.................... 89

Chapter IX: BUDDHOE'S CHRISTIANSTED IMPRISONMENT 95

Chapter X: MARTIN KING'S CHRISTIANSTED IMPRISONMENT................... 103

Chapter XI: BUDDHOE'S 1840 AND 1841 ARRESTS... 108

Chapter XII: CHRISTIANSTED'S TWO-DAY MASSACRE.................................... 112

Chapter XIII: BRAND CORPS MAJOR JACOB HEITMANN GYLLICH 127

Chapter XIV: THE GUNPOWDER 130

Chapter XV: LIST OF THOSE ARRESTED, ACQUITTED, SENTENCED
                 AND SHOT 135

Chapter XVI: BUDDHOE'S ASSASSIN (CARL LUDVIG CHRISTIAN
                 IRMINGER) 147

Chapter XVII: THE BRIG-OF-WAR "ØRNEN" 152

Chapter XVIII: GOVERNOR-GENERAL PETER von SCHOLTEN'S
                 PERSONAL LETTERS.. 158

Chapter XIX: ANNA ELIZABETH ULRICKA HEEGAARD 179

Chapter XX: VARIOUS LETTERS OF INTEREST 199

EPILOGUE...217

REFERENCES 221

ABOUT THE AUTHOR 229

INTRODUCTION

Join me as we take **A CLOSER LOOK** at our Emancipation of Monday, July 3, 1848. This was an extremely tumultuous time for those who kept order as well as those who participated. Freedom was taken and some knew not what to do with it (after having lived under chattel slavery all their lives). Every emotion known to man, like an adrenaline rush, was exhibited upon the declaration of freedom. Some cried, some danced, some prayed, some worried, some cursed, some jumped for joy, some were sad, some were scared, some were in disbelief…and, yes, some wanted revenge. Just imagine that moment!

When I endeavored on this project, I first decided to hold a class and teach the newly discovered and researched information in that manner, however, I was inspired by many to write this book instead. I wanted the information I had spent months researching and cross-checking to go out as "raw" as possible. No embellishments, no opinions, no additions, no subtractions….just the actual proven documentation that I had so passionately spent countless hours sifting through those thousands of pages, researching, downloading, copying and, most importantly, getting translated from Danish to English. This was very tedious work, as all the historical written records are hand-written in various handwritings and (some not-so-good penmanship, which we call "doctors' scribble") and others… well, a bit more readable. Then there were some pages I came across that had bled onto the previous page blotting out some of the information. I had to exercise a great deal of patience. Further, most of it was written in what is called "Gothic Danish." Luckily, I found two scholars in Denmark who could, with much effort, translate Gothic Danish to English.

We were always told just how fascinating, intriguing and unique our history was, but I found it even more so once I embarked on this extremely extensive research. Lots and lots and lots of surprises! It made me even more proud to descend from this heritage, and I'm almost certain it would do the same for all of you. I am delighted to share this treasure trove of what I consider to be "sacred" information.

So, come with me as we take **A CLOSER LOOK** at the Emancipation events, planning, activities, strategies, bloodshed, struggles, disturbances, disappointments, heroes….and the energy, spirit and mindset of the courageous enslaved African population on St. Croix who demanded and took their freedom against all odds **VICTORIOUSLY!!!!** I hope you share this work with your children, grandchildren….and beyond.

CHAPTER I

FREDERIKS FORT
EXAMINATIONS

THIS CHAPTER CONTAINS TRANSLATIONS OF COURT DEPOSITION testimony from persons arrested and questioned in Frederiks Fort under oath.

In this Chapter you will read the actual testimony of **GENERAL BUDDHOE, ADMIRAL MARTIN KING, MAJOR JACOB GYLLICH** and **FREDERIKS FORT COMMANDER CASTONIER** in their own words as translated from the military court in Frederiks Fort, protocol of justice documents.

You will also read where General Buddhoe requested of the court to leave the island and *"relocate to one of the English Colonies"* to which the court had no objection, and where he expressed to the court that he felt it *"would be dangerous for him to return to the Danish West Indies."*

You will also learn that Admiral Martin King never made it to Frederiksted town on the day of emancipation, but was stopped at Plantation Hogensborg, and that he at first did not at all believe emancipation was granted. You will also read in the translations where Admiral Martin King considered drowning himself at Negro Bay.

Translations of Major Gyllich's testimony before the court are included as it relates to both General Buddhoe and Admiral Martin King. The testimony of Decatur of Plantation Bethlehem is also included.

~~TESTIMONY IN THEIR OWN WORDS~~

~~~~#~~~~

John "General Buddhoe" Gottlieb

[The day was 1848 11ᵗʰ July, 7 o'clock in the morning]

After that, **the *Negro Gotlieb, also called Bordeaux*[1], previously from the Plantation Big La Grange,** appeared. After having been admonished to tell the truth, he explained that he never before Sunday afternoon had heard anything about that the movement for emancipation was taking place. But that day in the morning the Negro Charles from Butler's Bay came to him saying that tomorrow they should have their freedom, that the shells should be blown, and the bell should be rung in the night, that the negroes should go to the city in the morning on this occasion, and that everyone who unites with the whites on this occasion should have his head chopped off.

The night between Sunday [and Monday] the person questioned stayed at the plantation, until he, Monday in the morning, went to the city with all the others. He had at that time taken a saber, which he had borrowed from Henry from La Grange. In the city, he did not take part in any looting, but he has prevented this as much as possible. Monday in the afternoon and in the night, he was at the plantation.

Next morning, the person questioned took Mr. Beech's carriage and drove together with Isaac from Prosperity and Sambo from Wheel of Fortune and drove into all the plantations at the north side, and on that occasion, he introduced himself as "Captain" and enjoined all not to destroy the properties. The only Owner to whom he spoke was John Elliott at Hams Bay, and he said that he hoped there should be quietness between his people and according to his ability, his people, should feed his livestock and he give them allowance in the coming week. On this occasion, the person questioned admitted that Isaac from Prosperity had aimed his saber at Mr. Elliot in a threatening way.

When he came home, he heard that a gang of negroes passed by Little La Grange. They wanted to make trouble, and he stopped them and pacified them. After that time, he has been together with Major Gyllich. He asserts most definitely not having had any

---

[1]   General Buddhoe's name is spelled differently throughout the translations. For the sake of authenticity, I did not correct and/or change the various spellings of his name.

connection with Martin King before he, together with Major Gyllich, saw him at Slob, and he has not appointed any "Captain" or "Commanding Officer." He has appointed himself to "Captain," when he drove around, and already before Monday evening. He has never given any order to take the weapons away. It was between 9 and 11 o'clock Thursday that the person questioned joined Major Gyllich.

~~~~#~~~~

Major Jacob H. Gyllich

Appeared *Major Gyllich* who had been present during the previous explanation. He confirmed this as being true concerning himself. After that the Major explained that he had arrived at the Plantation Mt. Pleasant (Cohoun) when the destruction was over and when they were beginning to plunder.

Some barrels of sugar were outside the farmhouse, and while some people would prevent the crowd from attacking them, after the influence of Martin King, others would knock them apart. Among the last-mentioned, Decatur from Bethlehem particularly excelled. He was exceedingly violent and there is no question about his being most wild and violent, and he excited the others. He even resisted Martin King's order.

Bordeaux arrested Decatur the next day at Adventure. Bordeaux had heard that he had wanted to attack the sub-manager at Bethlehem. Bordeaux had also heard that Decatur had been a leader of the destruction of Mr. Moore's house.

~~~~#~~~~

General Buddhoe

Appeared *Gotlieb, called Bordeaux,* **from the Plantation Big La Grange**, repeating the explanation that he had given earlier (p. 32), and although he was examined for quite a long time, he would not admit that he knew more about the reason for the movement for emancipation than what he previously has admitted. Also, he denies having given any order whatsoever to get hold of weapons or having employed anyone as "captains" or "generals."

He admits having been around Tuesday morning to some plantations and having said there that the people should have allowance, but that they had to look after the plantation's livestock. He assured that he only had intended to take part in the movement that was supposed to produce emancipation.

The person questioned remarked to the protocol that he now wanted to leave the country and asked whether from the court's side anything was to object to this. The court remarked that in this case nothing was reported against him for which he could be held responsible according to the law.

The person questioned remarked further that he intended to go to one of the English colonies, and that he himself realized that under the present circumstances it could be dangerous to himself and the quietness of the colony to return. Because of that he was willing to commit himself not to return before he had informed either Major Gyllich or Chamberlain Rothe and had received answer from them. – Demitted. –

~~~~#~~~~

Admiral Martin King

[Anno 1848 24ᵗʰ July, the Commission established by terms of reference in Frederiks Fort began the meeting at 12½ o'clock. The two members of the Commission were present. The reference was produced under No. 12].

The arrested **Martin King** appeared, loose and free, previously belonging to the Plantation Bog of Allen. It is remarked that this arrested person, who generally in the country is supposed to be one of the head men in the movement which had preceded the disturbances and the lootings that followed last Saturday morning, had been apprehended and arrested. After having been admonished to confession and having been told that he, only by an open and complete confession, could avoid bearing the blame for the perhaps unfounded accusations that other accomplices may have done against him, he declared that he thought that the best thing he could do was to tell the truth and that he had decided to do so.

After that, he explained that he before Sunday evening, had not had the least knowledge about that some movement was to take place to effect the emancipation. That day's evening the arrested person was at Bog of Allen between 8 and 9 o'clock, and at that time he heard the bells ringing and the blowing of the shells. Also, at the mentioned plantation they began ringing the bell, but when the Manager had made sure that there was no fire, he forbade it and arrested some of the people.

Not until the arrested person shortly after arrived at St. Georges, where he has a wife, he learned that the noise was set out to achieve freedom. However, he says that he did not trust it very much or believe that it would be a success. The arrested person spent the night to Friday and Saturday at St. Georges. Early in the morning he went back to Bog of Allen. The people went to work, and the Manager ordered the arrested person to put the cart in order and drive to Westend. When the arrested person, together with Richard from Bog of Allen, arrived with the cart at St. Georges, the arrested person had gone away for a moment to collect his whip, and when he came back, people had arrived and had stopped the cart.

These people, among whom Phillipus from Mt. Pleasant and Decatur from Bethlehem, were violent, saying that the person questioned was not allowed to come to Westend and drove the cart into the sugar land. Although the person questioned opposed, while Phillipus slapped him on the arm with a "cutlass," he had to give in, and Richard brought the mules back to the plantation.

The mentioned Phillippus forced and persuaded the arrested person to follow him to the city, but when they came to the line which separates Mountain from Hogensborg, he got the opportunity to dodge and went back to the plantation, where he saw the Manager and stayed there all day, until he went to St. Georges in the evening to his wife, where he stayed with his wife until Saturday morning.

Then he went back to Bog, after having heard at St. Georges that it looked as if there was fire near Christiansted. Then he saw the Manager at Bog and told him about the fire, saying that he would go out to get information of it. He took a white horse belonging to Dewhurst and rode along the Centerline in the direction of Bass End and was not in any house on the way. When he had passed Diamond & Ruby, he met crowds coming back from Christiansted telling him that there had been fire near Herman Hill and that some people had been shot.

The arrested person turned around and rode back into Diamond & Ruby, where a crowd was destructing the managers' houses. The arrested person who did not arrive until the destruction was nearly over, talked to the negro Friday from Castle, whom he saw chopping up a beautiful chair. The crowd then ran to Strawberry Hill, but the arrested person, who all the time was sitting on the horse, did not stop at the last-mentioned plantation, but rode through. When he was asked, he says that the crowd which made the mentioned destruction was the same as he had met in the morning on the road to Christiansted and which had clashed there with the military, that these people did not have any leader, and that they had said that the reason for destructing the managers' houses was that they had gone to the city to shoot the negroes.

After that the arrested person rode to Barren Spot, where the destruction took place, but where the arrested person did not stop and did not make contact to anybody. When he was on the way between Slob and Clifton Hill, he sees that there were destructions at both places. The arrested person did not go to the last-mentioned place, but as a man from Slob came out to him on the Centerline, asking him to come in to protect his property, he rode in there. The arrested person was, until that moment, unarmed, but at the last-mentioned plantation he got a short saber from a man called Wilhelm from Bog of Allen. He tried to prohibit the residential building from being attacked, and he succeeded. The arrested person had nothing to do with the people who attacked the storage facilities.

A man called Andrew, who was in the house at Slob and who knew the arrested person, offered him some rum and water, and as he earlier already had drunk a little at home, he, who was not much used to rum, became agitated and somewhat drunk. It was here that Major Gyllich with his entourage met the arrested person. He thinks it was about 3 o'clock. Asked how the time from the morning at 9 – 9½ o'clock, when he left Bog of Allen, to 3 o'clock was spent, he remarked that he spent quite a long time outside Barren Spot, sitting at the wall there, and that he had been at Slob about an hour before Major Gyllich arrived there. At that moment he was, as he already has admitted, very much agitated. And when Major Gyllich came, the arrested person said to him that talking to the people was no use, blood had been shed in Christiansted, although no white people had been murdered, and the people wanted revenge, they wanted blood for blood.

When Major Gyllich after that said that if they wanted blood, they could take his, this made such an impression on him that he decided to do what he could to stop further destruction. Then he tried to mollify the negroes. He admits after a longer examination that he did not address Major Gyllich in his own name, and neither did he intend to scare him, though he admits that his behaviour in this situation was frank.

At La Reine, the destruction was nearly over and stopped when the arrested person arrived there with Major Gyllich. From there they rode to Glynn where everything was quiet; from there to Mon Bijou, where the same was the case; from there to Lucas Mt. Pleasant, where the residential house had been looted and the thieves were stealing the sugar. When the crowd there had become more quiet they rode to Jealousy, where nothing happened; from there to Castle, from where the arrested person with Major Gyllich and the entourage rode along the Centerline to the entrance to Bog, where the arrested person left him and rode to Bog and stabled the horse and then went to St. Georges where he spent the night.

The next day he did not leave St. Georges and Mountain and even participated in the protection of the first mentioned plantation, as it was under threat of attack, which many people will be able to testify, especially Becker "Johashy" Henry, the guard; the driver Ladjo and more. The next night the arrested person slept at Bog, and he spent the night alone in his house. In the morning many people saw him at this plantation, but when he learned that he was wanted, he escaped. He ran up into the hills behind St. Georges, where he spent some days hiding.

He denies having seen the negro Friday after the mentioned moment at Diamond & Ruby, which was between 11 and 12 o'clock Saturday noon. Also, he denies having ordered him to blow the shell or himself having been outside Upper Love on Wednesday morning when the looting took place there.

He kept hiding for three days in the bushes in the mentioned hills and lived from fruit and some bread which he had taken with him. In the night he went down to the gutter for water. As he eventually felt that he was wanted, he spent a day in another adjacent hill.

Besides bread for 20 Stuiver he received, when he first escaped, he has later bought for 2 Stuiver.

He has, in his despair, some days ago been down at Logan Negro Bay to drown himself. To take courage to this, he drank a whole bottle of rum but was, after all, not able to do what he intended and had to escape totally naked. But further up into the country, after having been naked for a whole day, he found a pair of trousers and a shirt which he put on.

One day when a military command of soldiers searched for him, he hid in a tamarind tree. Out of despair he decided to surrender to Mr. Newton and on the way to him he was apprehended.

[Read aloud [unclear]. Handed over to the arrest].

HOGENSBORG PLANTATION - 1838

**FREDERIKS FORT COMMANDER
FREDERIK JULIUS CHRISTIAN von CASTONIER**

9

**Chamber of Customs and Commerce Colonial and Trade Office.
On the Commission Appointed to Investigate the West Indian
Government Officials' Conditions on the Emancipation in 1848
and the Trial of Governor-General Peter von Scholten.**

Frederiks Fort Commander Frederik J.C. von Castonier

Your Excellency!

From our most humble report of this morning, Your Excellency will have learned that the condition on this side of the country is far from satisfactory. The garrison has been on their feet all the time for the last three days and has often been alarmed by false reports; but with assistance from 40 men which Capt. Irminger every day has given us from the brig's crew, we have more or less been able to endure the hardships.

In the middle of the country, the negroes committed the greatest excesses and held themselves in a distance from the fortress, as the larger part of those should be well disposed but they were held in fear by a few hundreds of bad subjects. I intend tomorrow early in the morning at precisely 4 o'clock to march from this fortress with two guns, 24 men infantry and 60 horsemen to Kingshill, partly to stop the possible unrest and partly to instill in the better people courage to resist by force the influence of the worse people. While I am away, Captain Irminger will take over the command of the fortress with 60 sailors and soldiers from the brig's crew together with some military.

To help in strengthening the defence, I have had to demolish the Royal Stable and the old bakery together with a large part of the old fortress garden that took away the view and the free firing on the north side of the road. If Your Excellency approve the excursions into the country carried out by me and let a similar demonstration be carried out from Christiansted, I have every reason to assume that it will have a beneficial effect on providing calm.

I have received some provisions from Captain Irminger, and I have already had to buy some in this city.

The Fire Corps has to-day been ordered out by the Vice City Major and is holding the eastern entrance to the city occupied. I shall have the honor of forwarding further information.

Frederiks Fort - 5 July 1848
3½ o'clock in the afternoon

Humbly,
Castonier

Your Excellency
Mr. General Governor v. Scholten
Grand Cross of Dannebrog and Dannebrogmand

At this moment we have been lucky to catch one of the head men.
[Produced during the examination 9 January 1849].

Flensborg.

~~~~#~~~~

Appeared Captain Chamberlain Castonier
The Fortress of Frederiksted.

A report from the person questioned concerning shooting in the fortress and the military etc. as well as the reports about the deficiencies in the fortress, dated 16 March 1847 and 6 May last year were produced and were laid ad acta under No. 40, 41 and 42.

The Appendix No. 40 reads as follows:

No. 40.

I have reason to believe, to be able to state without immodesty, that with the very frequent military excursions that I have made in the country and the constant attention that was paid to the smallest signs of unrest, has caused far fewer excesses and unrests to be committed in this jurisdiction than in Christiansted. So, 6th July, being present on the northside with a military force, I was the reason why the intended and partly-started looting of the Plantations Mount Stewart and Spring Garden was prevented.

The honored Commission will learn that in this jurisdiction (except for a negro boy who was wounded by Artillery Sergeant Frank with his escort that was sent here 6th July) nobody has been killed or wounded here, except for those that were sentenced by the trial court.

Frederiks Fort garrison 3 July 1848 were:

Of the Artillery:

9 Sergeants and Over Private First Classes

3 trained Over Private First Classes

24 Private First Classes

Of the Infantry:

2 Non-Commissioned Officers

16 men

A total of 54

Hence absent:

1 Non-Commissioned Officer at the Customs House

1 Private First Class (as guard of patient at the hospital)

2 trained Over Private First Classes (sent with messages to Christiansted)

1 Private First Class as Cook; and

1 DO, as opener by the civil arrestees

A total of 6

Rest

48 Non-Commissioned Officers and Privates for attendance of the 16 guns of the fortress and 23 pounds field guns.

/: The Infantry did not get here before 17th June :/

FREDERIKS FORT WITH WHIPPING POST

CHAPTER II

CHRISTIANSVAERN FORT EXAMINATIONS

THIS CHAPTER CONTAINS THE DEPOSITION TESTIMONY OF **CHRISTIANSVAERN FORT COMMANDER ANTON FALBE, FIRST LIEUTENANT ARNOLD MEINCKE** and excerpts from a historical account written by **ROYAL COUNCILLOR BERNHARD von PETERSEN** in 1855.

Major Anton Falbe was the Fort Commander at the Christiansvaern Fort during the time of Emancipation. He is buried in the Danish Cemetery in Christiansted. An image of his grave site and inscription is also included.

Lieutenant Meincke rode in the carriage with Governor-General Peter von Scholten as he made his way down to Frederiksted on July 3, 1848, along with Kammerjunker Rothe.

Royal Councillor Petersen was an eyewitness to General Buddhoe's imprisonment once Buddhoe was transferred from Frederiks Fort to Christiansvaern Fort. He also witnessed Buddhoe boarding the *Brig-of-war Ørnen* on Wednesday, December 14, 1848.

Christiansvaern Fort Commander Anton U. T. Falbe

*9 January 1849, the examination continued in the Government House, where then appeared Major in the Artillery, Chief of the Fortress of Christiansted, Knight of the Dannebrog **Falbe**, who explained....*

Already earlier that day Lieutenant Holstein had been ordered to go to Kingshill with a detachment. Before the General, as mentioned, went to the West End, he had given the person questioned the high command, and now during the afternoon, the person questioned let the eastern entrance to the city occupy by more than thirty men of the Militia Hunter Corps and a three-pound cocked cannon under the command of Lieutenant Rahr; the western entrance with more than thirty men of Christiansted's Division (the militia infantry) and also a three-pound cannon under Lieutenant McCutchin's command also, 25 men of the militia were sent to the prison outside the city to defend the access roads leading to Watergut, and with orders to keep up the communication and report to Lieutenant McCutchin.

All the chiefs were most seriously enjoined to, first with good, and then, if necessary, with force to prevent all negroes from penetrating into the city. However, reserves from the Fire Corps were lined up in the courthouse of Christiansted's Division, in the forecourt, in Hutchinson's yard, and of the West Indian Infantry in its barracks, to, if necessary, be used.

At sunset, the person questioned visited all the posts and found everything in good order everywhere, and everybody had understood their instructions. After that, the person questioned went to the General, who in the meantime had returned from the West End, and as it now was getting dark, and the person questioned found it necessary, in possible case at night, to have the sailors from the ships on land, he asked the General, to whom he had reported the other precautions taken, for permission to shoot alarm, which the General after some consideration gave him.

In the meantime, the negroes had started gathering on the line between Kingshill (the middle of the country) and Christiansted and they seemed to be approaching the city. The person questioned went, according to the orders that he had been given, to the fortress to command the shooting of alarm, which should make the "Center Division" and the part of the cavalry that had not come during the day, appear. But, just as the person questioned was about to command the shooting, Lieutenant Meincke appeared with orders from the General not to shoot. To this the person questioned answered that he at the moment had to obey, and that he reserved for shooting, if necessary.

Few minutes later, the person questioned heard shots fell from Lieutenant McCutchin's post, after which the person questioned at once let alarm be shot, and then at once the sailors from the cargo ships in the harbor appeared.

The content of General Scholten's report was presented to the person questioned concerning this issue, to the extent that it differed from the opinion of the person questioned, but the person questioned referred to what he said above, adding that he later had learned that the General had reproved McCutchin for having shot, because of which McCutchin had referred to the order, which the person questioned as Commander-in-Chief in Scholten's absence, had given him.

The person questioned must remark that he finds it absolute necessary that McCutchin did shoot, and he also thinks that he saved the city by this, as the crowds of negroes pushed forward a lot and had trash /: sugar straw :/ and other combustible material.

The alarm shooting effected that many women and children fled to the fortress and out onto the ships in the harbor. The night passed quietly, but fire was seen at some places in the country.

~~~~#~~~~

MAJOR FALBE GRAVESTONE, DANISH CEMETERY, CHRISTIANSTED

ANTON v. FALBE, Grave #60 (closest to the wall) "Far from his dear Home, here in the Lord's Peace our beloved Child ANTON v. "Slumbers" FALBE, Premier Lieutenant of the Artillery, Knight of Dannebrog. He was born on the 27th of May 1829 and ended his young, noble and prosperous life here. D. 2nd Nov. 1855. With the deepest pain, he is missed by parents and relatives."

First Lieutenant of the Infantry Arnold Johan von Meincke

[Anno 1849 11th January, the examination continued in the Government House].

Here, **Premier Lieutenant of the Infantry, Depot Officer** *Arnold von Meincke* appeared, and he explained that the first information he received about the outbreak of the unrest the night between 2nd and 3rd July, was from a messenger for the General, who woke him up immediately after the arrival of the General, who came from *Bülowsminde*.

The person questioned rose immediately and went to the General, with whom he met Captain Irminger and Major Falbe, and possibly a few others. Captain Castonier's report had at that time arrived, but no decision as to what should be done was taken, as the General was of the opinion that they were not sufficiently informed of what had been going on and that they had to get more information first.

However, Major Keutsch was told, together with a reliable negro, in all silence to try to explore the situation in the country in Christiansted's jurisdiction, and also a messenger was sent for the Police Master, Counsellor of Justice Andresen.

The General ordered him, with reliable negroes, discreetly, to examine the atmosphere in the countryside here around the city. Until Police Master Andresen's notification came, they discussed what could be done, and they also talked about sending the war brig to the West End, as Captain Irminger brought this topic up. But they did not reach any result as to what should be done, as the General all the time remarked that he had not got any reliable information as to what was happening. The person questioned himself had from the beginning all the time proposed to the General to let him ride out in a hurry to obtain accurate information, but the General would not agree to this. And, although he had the notification from Castonier, he repeated all the time that he could not see anything from this.

The person questioned did not know that the General the same morning by his coachman received a letter from his brother in Frederiksted, but finally, as the report arrived from Counsellor of Justice Andresen, the General decided to send the person questioned, together with Colonel de Nully, to the West End. But before that, they had been discussing if it would be correct that the General went there himself. However, the General had remarked that he would rather not do this, because he could possibly be forced to make promises that he would regret. Also, some persons, the person questioned does not know who, said that they might find to keep him down there.

The person questioned remarks that he in the night had been sent to Lieutenant Woods at the Militia Cavalry, who lived in this city, with orders to him to go to the General, who ordered him in all silence to gather the few cavalrymen living in this city, so that they could be ready, if necessary.

Later in the morning, almost the same order was given to Captain Mørck, who also was brought to the General, concerning the Militia Corps, Christiansted's Division, which he commanded. The person questioned does not know that there had been given any other order to Colonel de Nully, than that he had to bring peace, listen to what people said and inform the General about it. But it is most likely that he was ordered not to shoot at the negroes, for it was all about that from beginning to end.

As to what happened on the road to the West End and in the city, the person questioned referred to Colonel de Nully's explanation, which was read aloud to him, and which he also, for his part, approved, though with the remark that they, in Frederiksted's jurisdiction, saw larger and smaller crowds of negroes on the road, who all were on the way to Frederiksted, even though both Colonel de Nully and the person questioned admonished them to go home. And the person questioned has to add that he does not know what the Colonel had done or said as to the use of the cannons against the negroes, as he naturally had gone back to Christiansted, when this happened. For as soon as the person questioned had seen how things were in Frederiksted, he returned. But he does not doubt that it is as Colonel de Nully has said, for this man turned out, in spite of his advanced age, all the time from the beginning of the riot, to be a very determined, courageous and persistent man.

Like Colonel de Nully, the person questioned asked the various chiefs of the Militia Corps at the arrival at Frederiksted why their Corps were not gathered, for especially some people from the Fire Corps was seen among the mob. To this, several of them answered that the Vice City Stadhauptmand Chamberlain Scholten would not allow the shooting of alarm, and Major Logan remarked that his people had not been allowed by the negroes to leave the various plantations where they lived.

Seeing the negroes running about in the city with various flags, the person questioned asked an innkeeper called Robinson, whose house, by the way, had not been damaged in any way, from where these flags had come, and to this he answered that they had got them from him, and that they at once had torn the Danish flag into pieces.

As the person went to the city, Colonel de Nully ordered him to let Lieutenant Holstein with his detachment go on to Frederiksted, which he told Lieutenant Holstein, whom he found by the Plantation Diamond & Ruby, where he had stopped between Christiansted and Kingshill, and after that he reported this to the General at his return here.

When the person questioned after that went to Frederiksted together with the General, they met Lieutenant Holstein and his command on the road and it is possible that the General then renewed Colonel de Nully's order to them to go to Frederiksted.

As to Captain Castonier's report of 14th July, the person questioned must remark that it is correct that it is said in it that the long-requested sharp cartridges had not been received. When they were present in the fortress of Frederiksted January 1st last year, apart from 1,620 pounds cannon gunpowder and 699 pounds of musket powder, furthermore 925 sharp rifle cartridges, 576 sharp pistol cartridges and 2,658 sharp musket cartridges, of which quantity now the main part must have been left, when the unrests broke out.

On 1st June last year were required to the fortress of Frederiksted: 3,000 sharp musket cartridges, 5,000 sharp rifle cartridges, 250 sharp pistol cartridges and fifty 3-pound slant sacks for cannons.

The person questioned presented the requisitions, on which a delivery order has been endorsed by the Royal West Indian Government dated 14th June same year, and after that the requisitions were received in the depot 18th same month. But, 20th same month, they were returned to Captain Møller in Frederiks Fort with the request of adding information of the fineness of which the 3,000 musket cartridges should be, together with a remark that the garrison in Frederiks Fort usually made the cartridges that were necessary for Frederiksted's jurisdiction, especially for the fortress. The requisition was not returned from Captain Møller until 29th June.

After the person questioned arrival here with report of the situation in Frederiksted General Scholten decided to drive to the West End. But, before doing so, he received in the presence of the person questioned a letter from his brother by a negro, whom the person questioned had met, when he together with Colonel de Nully drove to Frederiksted. The negro had been on horseback near Frederiksted, and he had informed them that he had a letter to bring to the General. The letter contained a request in the name of all the inhabitants of Frederiksted, that the General, for God's sake, at once must come to Frederiksted, because otherwise there was danger of everything being destroyed.

After that the General at once got into the carriage together with Chamberlain Rothe and the person questioned went with him in the same carriage. Thus, it is a mistake, when the General in his report says that he came afterwards in another carriage.

At the entrance of Frederiksted, the negroes attacked the carriage with howls and screams demanding their freedom, mainly with these words: *"Massa, Massa, we must be free this moment, we have been waiting long enough for it,"* to which he at once answered: *"Yes, Yes, but you must go home and behave orderly"*[2]. He continued his way through the city to the fortress and drove into the yard of the fortress, the crowd storming after him to the gate of the fortress. In the yard, he got out of the carriage and went to the gate, or a little outside the gate, where he again shouted out to the crowd: *"NOW YOU ARE FREE, YOU ARE HEREBY EMANCIPATED, GO HOME, GO HOME,"* after which he went back to the fortress, which he did not leave until he later the same day drove back to Christiansted.

The person questioned, on the contrary, went out to induce the negroes to leave the square at the fortress, in which he succeeded. As the General, as above mentioned, were going to go to the West End, he decided to let the war brig go there. Just as the General

---

2   **This is in English. The text in the left margin is the Danish translation of it.**

in Frederiksted fortress was going to sit down at the table, it was reported to him that the negroes now had begun gathering in Christiansted's jurisdiction. He at once got into the carriage and went back to Christiansted, together with the person questioned.

When they arrived there, several planters and managers arrived, bringing the information that the negroes now gathered en masse and were getting nearer to the city. After that, the General decided to let alarm be shot, but when the order to that had been given, he sent the person questioned up to the fortress to revoke this order, as he said that he feared that the alarm should make the negroes riot at the distance.

When the person questioned had returned from the fortress, he followed the General to the western exit of the city, but when they were on the way there, the shots fell from Lieutenant McCutchin's post, and soon thereafter the alarm shots from the fortress. When the General had reached McCutchin's post, he stayed there, but ordered the person questioned as his adjutant to go out among the negroes to tell them that they were here, make them satisfied and make them go home. And as the person questioned had made the larger part go further away, on his way back he met the General and Attorney Bahneberg, both of them on horseback.

As to what, according to General Scholten's report took place Tuesday 4th July, the person questioned has essentially nothing to remark, except that as he together with the General rode from Big Princesse to this city over the land of the county, they were met by some negroes, who lamented some of their comrades, innocent people, had been shot, which caused the General, who thought that the shots had been fired from Colonel Holstein's detachment -- which turned out to have been the case -- to tell the person questioned that he was unsatisfied with this, saying that shooting at the negroes had been totally unnecessary.

On persistent request to do something to prevent the disturbances in the countryside, the General decided finally to send a command under Major Falbe Wednesday. And about noon the person questioned was sent out to get information as to where the command was and order it to return before night.

Thursday morning 6th July, when volunteers arrived from St. Thomas, the general disapproval over the fact that no force had been advanced against the negroes was uttered in violent and threatening expressions against the General, as well at the Customs House as in the Government House, as he had returned here from the first mentioned place.

As the person questioned found it most correct that something was done, he advised the General to, as soon as possible the same day, to send out a command, which with force could advance against the people who made the disturbances. The General finally decided to do so with these words: "Yes let them go," after in strong expressions having shown his ill-feeling against the Irishmen, "because it was the Irishmen who had wanted the shooting at the negroes, because these had broken the Irishmen's old bad furniture."

The person questioned now went away to give the necessary information to the person who should see to the fulfillment of the order and to do what was necessary to the equipment of the command.

Since that time, he did not see the General until 14th July, when he accompanied him to St. Thomas.

The person questioned is totally positive that the uprising could have been stopped at the beginning and the Emancipation could have been avoided just by smart and appropriately using the means that were available in the city of Frederiksted when the militia had been gathered in time and used together with the military force available in the fortress. For he thinks that the negroes, if that had been done, could have been kept out of the city.

Even more certain would their subjugation have been, if the war brig immediately had been ordered to Frederiksted, together with the force, which could be dispensed with from this city, where everything was quiet just as in the whole of the jurisdiction.

Gendarmerie Barracks in Christiansted at St. Croix, Danish West Indies [Destroyed by fire in 1914].

A HISTORICAL ACCOUNT ABOUT THE DANISH-WEST INDIAN ISLANDS ST. CROIX, ST. THOMAS AND ST. JAN – BY BERNARD von PETERSEN – 1855.

EXCERPT

It has still been stated that the highest number of negroes who could be assumed to be capable of playing an active part in an insurrection, on the condition that all agreed to this, would be 14 of the entire population. However, those who state this know little about the proper context of the case.

The women play a great part in the negro population. They work like the men and their entire build and size make them formidable opponents in hand-to-hand combat. They also proved more overbearing, more vengeful and far more passionate than the men, during the whole uprising.

With regard to the number of whites on the island, I have seen a list of the island's population in 1835 and, according to the same, there were then only 1,892 whites. Since that time, their number has decreased considerably. But let us also assume that the Caucasians and some free-coloured people who shared the thinking and interest of these, roughly constituted 2,000 souls.

The number of inhabitants in 1846 was 24,245 individuals. Deducting the 2,000 souls; leaves about 22,000 people left, who I assume would do everything in their power to force themselves into freedom one must see and not wonder that the slaves got their wishes.

It is, on the whole, difficult to explain that in the Year 1848, the year in which emperors and kings, with immense military resources consisting of the best troops in the world, having had to give in to revolutions and the lower classes', often unjustified demands, that this year one will wonder that some white people on a small island had to give in to an entire slave population that only demanded their freedom, which was unlawfully deprived of the freedom which is a right Christianity and civilization grant to every human being!

INSIDE COURTYARD - FREDERIKS FORT

CHAPTER III

OTHER DEPOSITIONS

THIS CHAPTER CONTAINS THE DEPOSITIONS OF *DECATUR* OF PLANTATION Bethlehem (*ROBINSON, STEVENS, FRIDAY and RICHARD BEECH*) all of whom gave short testimony related to Decatur. Also included is Police Officer *JOHAN CARL DOLLMAN, ALEXANDER KNOTT* (Manager of Plantation Bog of Allen); *RICHARD* of Plantation Bog of Allen; *JOHN McFARLANE* of Plantation Two Friends; *ROBERT* of Plantation Bog of Allen; *WILHELM* of Plantation Bog of Allen and *HENRY* of Plantation St. Georges.

Some of these witnesses corroborated the earlier testimony presented by Admiral Martin King during his examination. Additionally, Richard, Robert and Wilhelm were all members of Admiral Martin King's "Fleet" and from Plantation Bog of Allen.

In this Chapter we also have the testimony of *HOPE* of Plantation Granard, one of the Cavalry Officers in Christiansted.

We also have the testimony of two Janes (*JANE PETERSEN and JANE BUNTIN*), both of whom organized the "trash," "magass" or "bagasse" on the plantations to be carried to town, in case burning of the city became necessary.

The testimony of *JAMES W. SMITH* of the Fire Brigade is also included.

Decatur of Plantation Bethlehem

After that the arrested *Decatur* **from the Plantation Bethlehem** was produced, loose and free, to the court. The explanation given by Mr. Francis Newton was presented to him, concerning that the arrestee Decatur, Tuesday, had wanted to attack the Plantation Castle and that he, when he was chased back, had threatened to come back and put it on fire in the night.

Also, he denies Major Gyllich's explanation, and as it is said in this that he has been very violent, uncontrollable and agitating at Mt Pleasant. But he admits that he was present at the looting there.

He admits that he was in this city Monday and that he was in Mr. Moore's house when it was looted, but he assures that he did not act as written. On the contrary he admits that he took the money on the top shelf in the iron box. He cannot tell for sure how much money, but he thinks that there were about eight Doublons and six or seven bank notes. He kept the money, which he has not stored. He was arrested Wednesday.

[Read aloud and approved].

~~~~#~~~~

Brand Corps Officer Robert J. Robinson

Robert J. Robinson appeared, and on given occasion under offer of oath, he explained that as he, together with Major Gyllich and Mr. Beech, arrived at the Plantation Mt. Pleasant, the robbers, who had destroyed the farmhouse, were attacking some barrels of sugar outside the farmhouse.

The person questioned at that moment saw a negro, whom the others called "Decatur," being extremely wild, violent, and instigating. The arrestee Decatur was now presented to him, but although he seemed to recognize him as the person, he is not able to recognize him as the violent man, after which the arrestee was put back into the arrest.

~~~~#~~~~

John Stevens of Plantation Castle

The *mulatto John Stevens* **from Plantation Castle** appeared. He was admonished to tell the truth, and under offer of oath, he explained that in the afternoon Tuesday, Decatur and his brother Quammy, and also Benza from Bethlehem had arrived on horseback to

Castle, saying that this should be destroyed, and when they were prevented from doing so, they said that the whole country should be burned down. However, the person questioned and the other people at Castle made them go away.

As to the negro Friday, he says that it is true that he could prevent the destruction of the farmhouse at Castle, but he has been at the head of the squad and blown the shell for the gang who Wednesday in the morning attacked and looted the manager's house. Before the house was attacked, Friday stood at the head of the whole squad, blowing the shell and moving his hand towards the door of the manager's house, to signal that it could be attacked, and after that the squad rushed in.

The person questioned remarked furthermore that the negro Joshua from Lower Love was the one who first broke up the door to the basement.

~~~~#~~~~

After that, the **arrestee Decatur** was again presented, who was recognized by the previous person questioned, who repeated his explanation that Decatur had said that the buildings at Castle should be destroyed, and as this was prevented, exclaimed that it did not matter, because the whole of the country should be burned down.

~~~~#~~~~

John Stevens, after having been legally prepared, swore his statement, and after that he was allowed to leave. The arrestee was brought back from the arrest again.

~~~~#~~~~

Friday of Plantation Castle

The arrestee **Friday** was presented, and John Stevens' explanation as to him was presented to him. He admits that he blew the shell at the attack at the commission basement and the manager's house at Castle and that he gave the sign, mentioned by John Stevens, to the attack at these two places.

The arrestee declares that he did not know what he did, as he was wild and agitated.

[Johns Stevens was allowed to leave, and the arrestee Friday put into the arrest].

Lieutenant Richard Beech

Lieutenant Richard Beech appeared. Under offer of oath, he explained that he had been present at Mt. Pleasant together with Major Gyllich after the looting of the farmhouse, and as they would destroy the sugar at the works. Then he saw that the now presented arrestee Decatur, whom he is now quite certain to recognize, was extremely wild, violent and instigated the others to destroy. He behaved in such a way that his own first man, Martin King, could not control him.

After that, the witness swore his oath after having been legally prepared. -Dismissed-

~~~~#~~~~

Police Officer Johan C. Dollmann

Police Officer Johan C. Dollmann appeared and explained that he on the Saturday had seen the present arrested person Ferdinand from Prosperity smoking a cigar, and this person had told him that the fortress could be taken and blown up.

~~~~#~~~~

Alexander Knott, Manager of Plantation Bog of Allen

Alexander Knott, **Manager at the Plantation Bog of Allen**, appeared and explained that it was correct that the alarm was not heard at the Bog until the evening between eight and nine o'clock, and that the person questioned on that occasion arrested some individuals, and it was also correct that at that time there was no talk about emancipation at the plantation.

The person questioned remarks that he cannot say if Martin King was at the plantation at the mentioned time, but he supposes so and he will collect information as to this. As to what Martin King has explained about his presence at the plantation early Monday morning; about the episode with the cart; about that people from Mt. Pleasant and Bethlehem had stopped his cart and almost forced him to follow them along in the direction of Westend and that he had escaped from them between Mountain and Hogensborg and after that had come back to Plantation Bog and had told the person questioned what had happened, it is, all of it, correct and it is the same as the mentioned arrested person told the person questioned at that time. The person questioned does not know for sure, but does not doubt, that Martin King had spent the rest of the Monday at Plantation Bog until the evening.

The next morning, Tuesday, the negro Johannes, whom the person questioned had sent on an errand, came back at about 8½ o'clock, saying that he had met Martin King who had told him that Christiansted was on fire. Martin King must also had arrived at the plantation after that, although the person questioned did not see him and did not talk to him, even if Martin's explanation seemed to suggest so. Shortly after that, the person questioned himself left the plantation and so he does not know if it is true that Martin King had brought the horse back Tuesday evening or if he spent the night between Wednesday and Thursday at the Plantation Bog. The person questioned remarks that the negro Richard who had been brought as witness as well as Rose [?] and Wilhelm will be able to explain if Martin King was at the plantation at the times mentioned.

*[Here, three very unclear words, the last words meaning that
the person questioned was dismissed and left].*

~~~~#~~~~

Richard of Plantation Bog of Allen

The ***Negro Richard* from the Plantation Bog of Allen** appeared and was admonished to tell the truth, explained that he does not remember having seen Martin King at Plantation Bog Sunday. On the contrary, Martin King arrived Monday early in the morning and drove the cart, which should go to Westend, together with the person questioned. On that occasion Martin King did not talk about the day's events. What Martin King has told about the cart being stopped is true. He only remarks that there was only one man, Philippus from Mt. Pleasant, who with a saber in his hand threatened the person questioned to turn around with the cart.

Martin came back to Bog together with the person questioned later, that is about 10 o'clock. The person questioned did not see Martin, not until about eight o'clock in the evening, when fire was observed at the plantations on the northside. After that, the person questioned did not see him until Tuesday morning, when he arrived with the information that there was fire in Bass End. Then Martin took the white driving horse, and he and Johannes, who rode the other driving horse, left the plantation together.

In the evening about five o'clock the white horse was brought back by a boy, whom the person questioned does not know. Then the person questioned did not see him before Wednesday in the morning, when he came to the plantation, together with a man from St. Georges called England, and arrested two men, Samuel and Anthony. After that time the person questioned did not see him before he was arrested.

[Here, some very unclear words meaning that the person questioned was dismissed and left].

~~~~#~~~~

After that, a copy of the Police Journal of Frederiksted with the No. 13 concerning the confiscation of the false passport of the arrested **Charles of Oxford** *was presented. The passport in question was enclosed with the copy and presented with the No. 14.*

~~~~#~~~~

John McFarlane of Plantation Two Friends

After that, *John McFarlane,* **living at Plantation Two Friends** appeared. He was produced in court by the police. The passport was shown to him, and he admitted having written the same for a negro whom he did not know, and especially that he had signed it with the name standing on it, "I. Beckett," and that he knew that this was the name of the Manager of Plantation Oxford mentioned on the passport.

~~~~#~~~~

Robert of Plantation Bog of Allen

The *Negro Robert* **from Plantation Bog of Allen** appeared, and he explained, like the previous deponent, and remarked that he had not seen Martin Sunday evening, but on the contrary Monday morning, when he came to drive the cart, and when he came back afterwards. Further, did he see him Monday evening at Bog, when there was fire at the northside, and Tuesday morning when he came and took the white horse.

[Here, some very unclear words meaning that the person questioned was dismissed and left].

~~~~#~~~~

Wilhelm of Plantation Bog of Allen

The *Negro Wilhelm* **from Bog of Allen** appeared, and what he explained was completely consistent with the previous deponent, except that he did not think he had seen Martin King Monday evening.

[After that, the examination was postponed].

J. Rothe   *C. Sarauw*

~~~~#~~~~

Henry of Plantation St. Georges

The ***Negro Henry* from St. Georges** appeared, and he was admonished to tell the truth. He explained that he Monday morning, when Martin King was stopped with the cart, came to the place, seeing that him together with two other people from Bog, by a negro with bare legs partly were forced to following down in the direction of West End. He has also some time after that seen Martin King coming back to Mountain, and there he talked to him, at which occasion Martin seemed to be very startled, as the person questioned urged him to try to bring the sugar back to Bog.

~~~~#~~~~

Hope of Plantation Granard

Appeared the **tenant of the Plantation Granard, *Hope*,** last summer a member of the Center Division, now a member of the Cavalry Corps, who explained that as he Sunday July 2nd, after having been to church in this city, rode out to the Plantation Lowry Hill, he heard there that Major Logan should have said that the negroes would deny working the next day. Previously, he had not heard anything about riots breaking out, and he has no knowledge about the originators to this.

When tenant Elliot's explanation about him was presented to him, he remarks that he together with the mentioned Elliot, Elliot's brother, Percy and Nottage were commanded to various plantations, among others Castle Coakley, to arrest some negroes, but he did not enter this plantation, for while the others were there, he had gone to Diamond & Ruby to get his horse, and here he was to meet the others. So, he only heard only them talking about the utterances that should have been said at Castle Coakley, and especially Percy and Mr. Elliot told him about them. He has not heard similar utterances at other plantations.

As tenant John's explanation was presented to him, he remarks that he some weeks before the riot, from tenant Crosthwaite at Grove Place, had heard that there had been a gathering of negroes in the evening on the road between Grove Place and Upper Love.

Monday in the morning he drove into this city and learned on the way what had taken place at the West End. As he arrived here, he was ordered by the acting head of the

33

Center Division, Lieutenant Simmiolkjier, to try to gather 12 men of this company, and he procured that number and arrived with it in the afternoon to the square outside the fortress. Some of these men were under the person questioned, posted under McCutchin at the west entrance to the city, and the person questioned ordered the last mentioned to patrol every hour out on the road with two men.

When he so was out for the first time, he met tenant Kelly from the Plantation Herman Hill, with his under tenant, who told him that they had been chased away from the plantation, which is situated ¼ mile from this city, and the person questioned was ordered to report this to Major Falbe in the Government House. When he after that for the second time went out along the road, he met the crowds of negroes at Contentment, just outside the city and reported now to Major Falbe that the negroes were coming. At that moment it happened that General Scholten turned to the person questioned and asked him to tell McCutchin that *"he, for God's sake, must not shoot at his children."*

However, the General, together with Major Falbe, went to McCutchin's post, from where the shots, before they reached it, rang out. And as they arrived there almost at the same time as the person questioned, he did not report anything to McCutchin, but he went at once, after that, without hearing the General speak to him, out along the country road, where he saw the negroes retreating along the road to Orange Grove. However, the person questioned assumed that they would try to get into the city through another entrance, the Watergut, where there was no guard, and as he reported this to McCutchin. He was ordered with his staff from the Center Division to stand on the post here, where he took some negroes and stayed all night.

~~~~#~~~~

Jane Petersen

[This examination took place 21 February 1849]

After that, the ***Negro woman Jane Petersen*** appeared, and she explained that she Monday, 3rd July, when the negroes had made destruction in Didrichsen's house, saw a crowd passing her house going to the fortress square. Among these people was a lot of men and women carrying trash, threatening to set fire to the fortress. A woman called Jane Buntin was among them, taking some bundles of trash, which she placed outside the house of the person questioned, asking her to take it away so that others should not take it, which the person questioned did.

When she was presented with the Chamberlain's explanation about her, she remarks that the crowd of negroes did not stop at her house, and the crowd had not tried to set fire on the trash, neither had she seen them having matches or other such things for making fire.

*[Read aloud in the English language and approved by
the person questioned, after which she left].*

~~~~#~~~~

Jane Buntin

After that, the **Sambo Negro woman Jane Buntin** appeared, explaining that she Monday, 3rd July, about 12 o'clock, saw a large crowd of negroes going into the city past her house. They carried trash from the works ["værk"][3] and matches, threatening to set fire to the city. She tried to turn them from their purpose, and for this reason she followed them to the house of the previous person questioned, outside which they threw quite a lot of trash, which she told Jane Petersen to collect and carry into her yard, which she did.

She adds that when the crowd of negroes saw all the things that had been thrown out from the house of the City Bailiff and the court archives, some of them said that now they too would have some fun burning the city down, and also some of them said that they wanted to set fire to the fortress, and that should be close to the so-called "Magazine," where there is a horse stable.

[Read aloud in the English language and approved, after which the person questioned left].

~~~~#~~~~

James W. Smith of the Fire Brigade

[This examination took place 21 February 1849]

[A copy of the letter from James W. Smith is enclosed].
After that the person questioned explained that the negro Buddo, in the days when the disturbances took place on this island in the past summer, for his own safety, stayed in the Fire Brigade's Guard Room in this city, and here the person questioned got to know him.

As Buddo, towards the end of July, was to go from here to Tortola and he said that he had no acquaintances there, the person questioned gave him the now-produced letter of recommendation to a man whom the person questioned knew on that island.

---

3   The "works," also called "the factory" consisted of the mill, the curing house, the cooking house and sometimes a distillery.

It was a joke that he in this letter called Buddo "General Governor," and the reason for that was that the men in the Fire Brigade used to call him that, because he got so many negroes in as arrestees. Because after that the emancipation had been granted, Buddo was immediately on the white people's side.

The person questioned did not know that the negroes called Buddo "general," but he knows that a song has been made by the negroes, in which he is called this.

The person questioned had not heard anything about the disturbances in the countryside until Sunday, 2nd July in the afternoon after 8 o'clock, and he stayed the whole night at home with his wife, who was ill after having given birth. Neither Monday nor Tuesday was he out in the city but stayed in his house or very close to this.

Wednesday he appeared on summons with the brigade. He assures that he does know the least about from where the negro movement originated, and he had never had much connection with Buddo before the disturbances broke out. And he wrote this letter in youthful light-headedness when he saw that many others took care of Buddo. He also thinks that it will appear from the letter that it was mostly written for fun.

Besides, he wanted to make it known that, because of Buddo, no blood had been shed and the city had not been burned down, as he tried to influence the negroes and make them refrain from violence.

What he says about Moore is what he has heard rumors about, and what he mentions as having happened Tuesday, 4th July is a writing mistake for Monday 3rd July.

The reason for his mentioning that he has known Buddo as slave is that he, previously sometimes, has come to the person questioned to buy cigars, and he assures that he did not know him better, which he is willing to swear.

The Major, whom he mentions in the letter which he gave Buddo is Gyllich.

[Read aloud in the English language to the person questioned and approved by him, after which he left].

~~~~#~~~~

ST. CROIX MAP (WITH DESIGNATED NINE QUARTERS IN RED)

QUARTERS ARE: WEST END, NORTHSIDE A, NORTHSIDE B, PRINCE, KING, QUEEN, COMPANY, EAST END A and EAST END B.

CHAPTER IV

EYEWITNESS NARRATIVES

THIS CHAPTER CONTAINS THE NARRATIVES AND PHOTOGRAPHS OF TWO eyewitnesses to the Emancipation events: ***FREDERIK von SCHOLTEN*** (the Governor-General's brother who lived in the vicinity of the Customs House) and ***CARL LUDVIG IRMINGER*** (the Captain of the *Brig-of-war Ørnen*). These narratives outline the eyewitness and participatory perspectives of the Emancipation events before and after Emancipation Day by these two Danish officials.

Frederik von Scholten was the Vice-Stadthauptmand and Customs Inspector in Frederiksted during his brother's governorship. Frederik was approached about the plantation fires and conch shell blowing on the Northside estates on the night of July 2, 1848, but did not become alarmed.

Frederik von Scholten was born on April 8, 1796, in Copenhagen and died on December 22, 1853 on St. Croix, at the age of 57. He is buried in the Lutheran Church Yard Cemetery in Frederiksted. An image of his grave site is included.

Captain Carl Irminger was the Captain of the *Brig-of-war Ørnen*. Irminger also participated in a "cabinet meeting" with the Governor-General on the day of Emancipation but was hindered and discouraged from taking the *Ørnen* to Frederiksted prior to Emancipation being granted.

FREDERIK von SCHOLTEN

NARRATIVE OF THE INSURRECTION OF 1848
BY FREDERIK von SCHOLTEN

Frederik von Scholten was a younger brother to the Governor-General and Customs Inspector in Frederiksted. He also had the position of Stadthauptmand, which meant that it was his responsibility to call in the local militia in times of emergency. He was thus in close touch with developments almost from the outbreak of the riot, and he gives us a play-by-play account of the happenings.

In the week that preceded the 3rd July 1848, I was confined to my bed with rheumatic swelling in my right hand. On Sunday the 2nd July I felt a little better and could more or less use the hand. On the afternoon of that day I received a visit from one of our most respectable planters. In the course of our conversation, he told me that there were strange reports in circulation concerning the negroes, who, it was said, were to refuse to go to work on the next day, and to demand their freedom. He could not assign any further grounds for these reports than hearsay. Being accustomed to hear of war and revolution in Europe, as well as disturbances and riot in the French islands, from the fact of the majority in this little place, Frederiksted, seeking to make up for the monotony of their existence by spreading and listening to all sort of idle rumors and scandals, this information made no further impression upon me. I bade him, in the meantime, to acquaint the Commander of the fort, and the Police Master with what he had heard, and promised myself to inform my brother the Governor-General, as soon as he arrived here in the "*Ørnen*" a brig of war, which was momentarily expected. At about 8 o'clock in the evening my physician came to attend to me, and he spoke of the alarming reports that were in circulation. As he appeared to be somewhat concerned about the matter, I remonstrated with him and spoke of the evil of spreading such reports, which, if unfounded, might awaken ideas among the slaves which it was to the interest of everyone to prevent. Not that I feared that they would be disposed to violence or riot. They had been generally well treated and were apparently satisfied.

About 9 o'clock, I received a message that the Governor-General had arrived in Christiansted, and that his carriage which stood in my yard was to go up there, but as it was late, I gave orders to the coachman to wait until the next day. In the meantime, I went to bed. A short time after, my servant told me that there must be a fire in the country as the bells were being rung and shells blown. As this is the customary manner of giving notice of such, the thought of anything unusual did not occur to me. And as I could see no sign of any fire from my house, which is built on an elevation, I concluded that it was upon a distant estate, and again sought refuge in sleep.

This lasted but a short time, when I was once again aroused by a loud knocking at my gate. Opening the window, I immediately recognized the voice of the Brand Major commanding in Frederiksted. He told me that the negroes in the country were rioting and desired their freedom, and that was the reason why the bell ringing and blowing of shells were to be heard. We then spoke about the plan of action we should adopt, and whether the alarm gun should be fired or the Brand Corps and militia should be called out. The Major, having stated that the negroes were committing no excesses and only making a disturbance, I looked upon this as a good sign, for when one has evil designs, he rarely makes a noise, but generally proceeds to action at once. Nevertheless, it was a doubtful point with me whether I, as Stadthauptmand, would be justified in firing the alarm, the militia law not stating anything definite or to the point as to who should give such an order. On the other hand, my authority only extended over the militia. Over the Fort, from which the alarm gun should be fired, I had no command whatsoever.

There were many considerations which induced me to proceed with caution in the matter. To have fired the alarm would have been equivalent to placing the island in a state of siege. The power to do this rested only with the Governor. Moreover, such an act would have summoned the whole of the white population into town, away from their estates, leaving their wives, children and old women in the power of the negroes. With no one to check on them, had excesses been committed, how blameable it would have been to have acted so precipitately. I was confirmed in this opinion by a planter and military officer, who shared my views on the subject. The officer remarking that: *"Should the negroes be intent on evil, they could easily prevent isolated members of the militia from coming in, and should the opposite be the case, he saw no reason for calling them from their estates, where they might by their presence be able to check violence and plunder."* The Police Master Andersen, coincided with these views, observing; "let us not by hasty proceedings provoke the negroes. The bell-ringing and noise do not indicate that they are intent upon violence. We must proceed with caution if we do not desire to see things worse." These words from one who had a large experience of the character of the negro, carried weight with most of us.

The opinion has since been expressed on more than one occasion, that the Brand Corps, which was composed of free-coloured people, should have been called out, but from prudential motives it was deemed advisable to limit their action until absolutely necessary. I shall now attempt to picture the events which followed:

About two o'clock a.m., eight or ten mounted militiamen came in from the country and informed me that the condition was such as the earlier reports had stated. That there were noisy demonstrations and disorder, but nowhere had actual violence been committed. These gentlemen had left behind them their wives, mothers and children, so to speak, in the power of the negroes, without the least fear that that they would be exposed to any kind of danger. They came to inquire if the alarm gun had been fired, and if such were the case, to meet as accustomed. I explained to them that the gun had not been fired, as it was not considered prudent to call them away at such a moment from their property, where they could best work to preserve order. They therefore returned to their homes.

At four o'clock a.m., I sent off my brother's carriage to Christiansted, and by same opportunity a letter in which I described to him the condition of things in Frederiksted. At the same time expressing the hope that order and quiet might be restored by representations and negotiations.

At 7 o'clock in the morning the negroes streamed into the town in large numbers. Shortly afterwards it was reported to me that the police office was being plundered and demolished. The Second Brand officer, who was with me, after expressing the opinion that it was in no way advisable to call out the Corps, undertook with some of the best disposed of his men to assist in the keeping of order. And it is but fair to say, that it was owing to the activity and representations of the free-coloured men that more violence was not committed, only three houses being plundered and wrecked.

At about this time a negro came crying to me and begged me to write a letter to the Governor-General asking that he would come down to Frederiksted as soon as possible, so that by his presence, he might save the town from further molestation. With this I joyfully complied beseeching my brother not to delay as only he would be able to quiet the negroes. In the meantime, the Brand Major had narrowly escaped with his life. Riding into town from his estate he was attacked by the negroes, a negro woman, striking at his neck with an axe, which fortunately glanced off without injuring him. To show that he intended them no harm, he threw away his sword, exclaiming: "Take my life, if that can satisfy you, I come not as an enemy, but as a friend!" With these words they seemed impressed and allowed him to pass on his way.

A crowd of negroes came shouting and yelling up the street, and stood in front of my residence, demanding that I should proclaim their immediate freedom. Representing to them how wrongly they had acted by destroying and plundering, I advised them to keep quiet until the Governor-General arrived, as he alone could satisfy their demands. Seeing that they were now more peaceable, I went to the Fort where several of the inhabitants of the town had assembled. These were most restless, not to say, unreasonable. Some thought that to save the town from further disturbance, I should, in the Governor-General's name, have declared the negroes free, but as, in my opinion, I had no such power, I could not, nor would not, take it upon myself to do so.

Nevertheless, it was the opinion of everyone that only the prompt emancipation of the slaves would save the island from further destruction. And now a considerable number of negroes had assembled together in the Fort yard. They cried and shouted, demanded their freedom, and called on the soldiers to fire upon them. This the Commander of the Fort had some difficulty in preventing. Many who were present begged him also not to do so, as the town would surely be burnt to ashes. Of this, there could not be any doubt, as near by, behind a corner house, which could not be commanded by the guns of the Fort, there were several negro women gathered together with "trash" or dry cane leaves, which, as the first shot from the Fort, it was arranged they should light and throw into the doors and windows. The fire would thus have spread quickly through the town, as the houses were mostly deserted, and there was no one to check it. With a view of quieting the threatening multitude, I went among them, accompanied by the Catholic priest and a few of the bravest of the inhabitants. The priest, whose influence was very great, spoke to them, admonishing and exhorting them to be quiet.

On the other hand, on my addressing myself to one who appeared to be a leader of them, I received the following reply: *"Massa, we poor negroes cannot fight with the soldiers, as we have no guns, but we can burn and destroy if we do not get our freedom, and that is what we intend to do."*

It was rumored in the Fort that the negroes intended to storm it, and for that reason had procured an English flag, which they regarded as the symbol of freedom. I myself saw the flag in the crowd, and nearing the flag-bearer after some difficulty, I asked the young negro why he did not carry the Danish instead of the English flag, to which he answered: *"Any flag is good on such an occasion."* But on my speaking further he seemed visibly embarrassed and moved away among the crowd. About ten o'clock a.m. a great noise was heard in the upper part of the town. Some said it was the Governor-General, but it turned out to be the Stadthauptmand of Christiansted, Oberst de Nully, and the Governor-General's adjutant. The Oberst stepped out of the carriage and spoke to the crowd, which was so dissatisfied that the Governor-General had not come himself that they would not listen to him.

Suddenly, there was a great movement among them, and with repeated cries of *"Moore!" "Moore!"* they rushed down the Strand-street. Here, the infuriated mob commenced immediately to plunder and destroy Merchant Moore's store and residence. Mr. Moore himself sought refuge on board one of the vessels in the harbor. The cause of this unexpected outbreak is said to have been brought about by Mr. Moore's carelessly speaking to the negroes, who understood that he would request the garrison of the Fort to shoot them down. This would have been an easy matter, for it was quite possible to sweep the street with a couple of field guns from the water battery and the Fort gate; but the Commander of the Fort was besought not to fire for fear that in their desire for revenge the negroes would burn down the town and destroy every white person who might fall into their hands. Besides, as the actually guilty ones were in Mr. Moore's house, plundering, only innocent people who were in the streets would have been killed.

Several sailors from the English vessels in the harbor were now to be seen among the excited people, encouraging them by words and actions. And particularly conspicuous upon the wharf were several water casks belonging to these vessels, on which was written in large letters – 'LIBERTY!' It is worthy to remark, in contrasts to these proceedings, that the free-coloured population did their utmost to prevent the negroes from breaking into the houses and warehouses in the vicinity.

Most of the whites were now either on board the vessels or in hiding. About this time a negro appeared upon the scene, who seemed to be in command of the immense concourse of people who filled the street. This was Buddhoe, or as he was called later on, "General Bourdeaux."[4]

About three o'clock p.m., the Governor-General arrived, accompanied by Kammerjunker Upper Court Assessor Rothe. The General stepped out near the Fort, went in among the crowd and declared the negroes to be free. He then requested Kammerjunker Rothe, and as far as I can remember, Major Gyllich, the Brand Major, to see that the negroes left the town, which these gentlemen soon accomplished.

Later on, a detachment of troops arrived from Christiansted, and at five o'clock p.m. the Governor-General returned to Christiansted, after having ordered the cavalry, which had recently arrived, to go back again. First Lieutenant v Holstein, with two pieces of cannon and forty men, remained overnight in the Fort.

The brig-of-war *Ørnen* Captain Irminger, arrived in the harbor shortly before sunset. The night passed quietly enough, though fires illuminated the hills of the north side. On Tuesday, the 4th of July, a number of negroes were seen on the road leading to the north side, and it was feared that, should they enter the town, it would doubtless result in bloodshed or incendiarism. In order to prevent this, Major Gyllich rode out among them and, by repeated assurances that they were now free and would not be brought back to slavery again, succeeded in inducing them to return to their homes. At the same time he persuaded the negro Buddhoe to accompany him to town, a wise move, for it was through this negro's influences over them that order and quiet were restored to this part of the island.

In the meantime, Kammerjunker Rothe, the Vice-Brand Major and a prominent planter went to Annaly and Spring Garden, while Major Gyllich, Buddhoe, or General Bourdeaux, and two of the most respectable free-coloured burghers went to the south side.

---

[4]   He had obtained this brilliant military title on account of his fantastic attire.

The company in which I found myself arrived first at Estate La Grange. We had little difficulty in getting the negroes together, who stood around our carriage as Kammerjunker Rothe read out and explained the Proclamation to them. Continuing on the road, we came to Estate "Northside," where we met with the owner and his family who had remained there during the whole tumult. They told us that during the forenoon of the same day, they had been attacked by the negroes from the neighbouring estate of Ham's Bay, who under the pretext of wanting to take the overseer's weapons from him, attempted to force the dwelling house. The negroes of the estate defended them and prevented the intended violence.

From that place we went to Ham's Bay where we found it difficult to collect the negroes, who had forced the owner and his family to take flight in the fishing boat shortly before. After having restored something like order among them, we returned to Frederiksted.

The expedition in charge of Major Gyllich after visiting 20-odd estates, reached as far as La Reine. Mr. Beech read the Proclamation on each of them. On the road they learned that there was a large gathering at Estate Slob, which had been doing a great deal of plundering and destruction. Though Buddhoe declared that he did not know the negroes on that part of the island, and it was remarked that Estate Slob was outside of West End jurisdiction, Major Gyllich decided to go there, being under the impression that he might prevent further troubles.

Going up the hill towards Slob they met a man named Martin King, Chief of the "Fleet," as they called this meeting. This negro, who was half drunk and riding a white horse, and who seemed to be a leader among the crowd which they encountered, upon understanding the object of the expedition, after a great deal of outrageous and foolish talk, yielded to the representations of the Major, and by the influence he seemed to wield over the rest of the his comrades, was of great assistance in restoring order among them. After visiting Estates La Reine and Mount Pleasant, the Major and his party returned to Frederiksted.

On Tuesday and Wednesday several planters with their families came into town and sought refuge on board the ships in the harbor. The owner of the Estate Negro Bay, with twenty or thirty other managers and overseers also came in, an error which resulted in his estate being plundered. By this time prisoners were being continually brought in. The negroes bringing them in themselves. To this Buddhoe mainly contributed.

On Thursday morning at four o'clock a considerable force consisting of two cannon, infantry and cavalry under the command of Captain v Castonier left the town. In the meantime, the Fort was garrisoned from the brig-of-war. Though this expedition met with no opposition, it served a good purpose, as from that time perfect quiet and order were brought about.

Frederik von Scholten Grave Site, Holy Trinity Lutheran Church Frederiksted

Grave #1

"HER UNDER HVILER FREDERIK v. SCHOLTEN, CAPITAIN AF DEN DANSKE
S0ETAT, KAMMERHERRE RIDDER AF DANNEBROGE OG AF DEN FRANSKE
AERES LEGIONS ORDEN M.M. F0DT D. 8 APRIL 1796, D0D D. 2 DECEMBER 1853."

In English the inscription reads:

"HERE LIES FREDERIK v. SCHOLTEN CAPTAIN OF THE DANISH
NAVY, CHAMBERLAIN KNIGHT OF DANNEBROG AND OF
THE ORDER OF THE FRENCH LEGION OF HONOR ETC. BORN
THE 8 APRIL 1796, DIED THE 2 DECEMBER 1853."

PLANTATION LA GRANGE - 1834

CAPTAIN CARL LUDVIG CHRISTIAN IRMINGER

50

NARRATIVE OF THE INSURRECTION OF 1848
BY CARL LUDVIG CHRISTIAN IRMINGER

After a stay of several days in the island of St. Thomas, Governor-General v Scholten sailed in the forenoon of the 2nd July 1848, for St. Croix, in the *brig-of-war "Ørnen,"* which I commanded.

About four o'clock in the afternoon we anchored in Bassin (Christiansted), suspecting nothing of the row which the negroes intended to make. The General dined with me. At sunset he landed in order to proceed to *Bülowsminde,* and as he heard that I intended to have the ship painted, he invited me to pass the time at his beautiful country seat. About 10 o'clock, p.m. we retired to rest.

The 3rd July at about two o'clock in the morning, I was awakened by the General's servant with a request that I would come to the General as quickly as possible. I immediately repaired to his presence and found him already dressed. He then showed me a report from the Chief Commander of the Fort in West End (Frederiksted), Captain v Castonier, which stated that the negroes were restless at that part of the island—that bells were being rung on the estates—and they were sounding the alarm on their shells (conch shells).

When I had read the report, the Governor-General said: *"what is now to be done?"* To this I answered that I thought the best thing to do was to seek as quickly as possible to smother the disturbance at its birth, because every minute now lost would lend additional strength to the disturbers of the peace. It was my impression that twenty to thirty armed men should immediately be sent on horseback to West End in order to scatter the negroes apart.

The Governor remarked that he could not dispose of such a force. I replied that I did not think it would be so difficult to get such a number of mounted militia collected from the nearest estates.

In the meantime, the General's horses were saddled and we now both rode, accompanied by a mounted servant, down to the Government House in Bassin. The night was a starry one and the weather exceedingly fine. We stopped now and then on the tops of the different hills which we rode over to listen if we could not hear the blowing of shells or any shouting. But all was hushed, and we heard only the rustling of the cocoa-nut palm leaves moved by the trade wind. As soon as we arrived in town, messages were sent to Major v

Falbe, who was Chief of the Fort in Bassin, Major v Gjellerup, who lived in the barracks, Oberst de Nully, Major Keutsch and others. We now spoke of what was to be done. I still maintained that action should be taken immediately and that if the cavalry force which I had asked for could not be got, which I could by no means admit, other military must immediately be sent to West End.

I furthermore said to the General that I would go on board to let the men that could be dispensed with get ready to land, and, at the same time, get the *brig* ready for sea so as to be able to leave for West End by daybreak, if ordered. The General requested me to remain a little longer in the Government House so as to avoid making any disturbance in town where all was still and quiet. The conference ended, I believe, in Major Keutsch's coachman being sent towards West End for more information as to how it stood with the island. It was now nearly five o'clock in the morning. The time passed and nothing was done. I believed I knew the negro character, and that the riot could have been smothered at the beginning by decisive action. Seeing that my presence at Government House was of no further use, I told the General that I would now go on board, so that I could get the brig ready for sea, and to send armed men on shore, if required. This I did and awaited the General's order.

To my surprise I received none whatsoever, and about eight o'clock a.m. I again went on shore. There I was informed that Oberst de Nully and Lieutenant v Meincke had been sent to West End. I also found some soldiers drawn up and ready to set out, though I afterwards learned, with orders not to go farther than Kingshill (an estate in the middle of the island). Interrogating the General as to whether the brig should not sail to West End, I received the answer that she might be possibly required in Bassin, and I would receive further orders.

In Bassin, everything was quiet, and I began to believe that the whole affair did not mean much. Indeed, scarcely anyone seemed to have any knowledge of it. I then informed the General that everything was ready as well for sea, as to send men ashore, and should the General have anything to order, I could be found in the Athenaeum (a reading room nearly opposite the Government House).

About one o'clock p.m., Lieutenant v Meincke arrived from West End and reported the state of affairs. He brought at the same time information that the negroes wanted to speak to the Governor-General himself. General v Scholten had the horses immediately put to, taking Kammerjunker Rothe with him into the carriage to drive to Frederiksted. This man, from what I had heard, had been always an advocate for the emancipation of the negroes. Before the General drove off, I requested a decisive order from him as to whether I should remain lying in Bassin or depart for West End. After some reflection, he gave me the order. With this I left for that place.

On my arrival, and immediately after having anchored, the "*Ørnen's*" boats were armed and I went ashore. The King's Wharf was full of negroes, and everything was in disorder. Accompanied by some of my armed men, I went to the Fort. By the entrance to same, I met General v Scholten in his carriage, he was just ready to drive back to Bassin. I reported my arrival and asked for orders. The General's answer was: "I have given emancipation. Remain here with the *Ørnen.*"

This was the last order I received from him, and I did not see him again before my arrival in Denmark in the following year.

In the Fort, I spoke with Captain v Castonier, and shortly after, I sent, according to agreement with him, an officer with about fifty men as a reinforcement as well as for patrolling. This detachment remained ashore some time.

"By this time nearly all the estate negroes had left the town. Still everything was in the greatest confusion. Town Bailiff Andresen's house and Police Assistant Didrichsen's were entirely wrecked by the negroes. A Mr. Moore's house and store had suffered to the extent of 20,000 dollars. Several lesser excesses had been committed, and armed negroes were seen, off and on, riding through the streets at a gallop. Most of the whites had fled to vessels lying in the harbor, of which the "Johann Marie" had over two hundred fugitives on board. On the night of our arrival, fires illumined different parts of the island."[5]

As everything was yet in the greatest confusion, and deeming it of the utmost importance to bring about order, Vice-Stadthauptmand F. v Scholten, the Commander of the Fort, Captain Castonier, Police Master Ogaard and myself, assembled, and after due deliberation, issued the following order:

[5] **Extract from Captain Irminger's Report to the Minister of Marine. Dispatched 12ᵗʰ July 1848.**

"It is hereby made known, for the information of everyone concerned, that in case the country people should come to town in a riotous way and threaten to attack the Fort, or otherwise to disturb the inhabitants, then, and in such case, where more than ten people are collected together, the Fort is ordered to fire upon them, as also his Majesty's brig-of-war Ørnen. All peaceable inhabitants are therefore desired not to interfere with the country people but keep out of their way."

Frederiksted, 4th July 1848

At the same time, the Proclamation of Emancipation that had been sent to West End from Bassin was read out. It is as follows:

1. *All unfree in the Danish West Indian Islands are from to-day free.*

2. *The estate negroes retain for three months from date the use of the houses and provision grounds of which they have hitherto been possessed.*

3. *Labour is in the future to be paid for by agreement, but allowance of food to cease.*

4. *The maintenance of the old and infirm, who are not able to work is, until further determined, to be furnished by the late owners.*

The General Government of the Danish West Indian Islands, St. Croix, the 3rd July 1848.

P. v Scholten.
(L.S.)

Still the greatest disorder reigned in the country, and there was much plundering and destruction on the estates. In the meantime, many negroes showed that they themselves wished for peace and order, so much so, that several of the originators of the disturbances were caught and brought into the Fort by the friendly-inclined negroes.

On the 5th July, the condition of the country being about the same, and as several buildings, together with a large garden planted with coconut trees near to the Fort obscured the view and prevented firing from the Fort in that direction, it was found expedient to demolish them. This was soon effected by the brig's indefatigable crew, so that we could now cover the Northside road from the Fort.

There were now forty to fifty men from the brig almost continually in the Fort as a reinforcement. As it was then found necessary to undertake military excursions inland to overawe the negroes, and at the same time to secure the authors of the riot, I took over on the 6th before daybreak the command of the Fort and garrisoned it with the crew from the brig. At four a.m. all the Royal Infantry and Artillery, together with the planters, overseers and managers of estates, marched off under the command of Captain v Castonier. The latter force alone amounted to forty horsemen and from sixty to seventy foot.

At noon Art. Lieutenant Frank arrived from Bassin with a detachment of militia cavalry. Immediately after, a report was circulated that the Governor-General was dying, and on that account a Provisional Government had been organized in Bassin. I asked Lieutenant Frank if he know anything about it, to which he answered that shortly before he had left Bassin, he had seen the General on the wharf.

Some time after, Kammerjunker Rothe arrived in a boat from Bassin and read aloud the following:

"On account of the illness of the Governor-General, and with his concurrence, have we, the undersigned, Govt. Councillor Kunzen, Govt. Councillor Petersen, Kammerjunker Lands-overrets Assessor Rothe, Justitsraad Lands-overrets Assessor Foester, Justitsraad Police-master Frederiksen, Kammer Assessor Arnesen, and Lawyer Bahneberg, assembled as a Governing Commission, with full power to take all steps necessary in the present disturbed condition to bring about peace and order in the country.

The command of the military will be taken over by Oberst P. de Nully and Major A. v Falbe, who will confer with the above-named Commission, if necessary."

> *St. Croix, Christiansted,*
> *6th July, 1848*

KUNZEN   *C.B. PETERSEN*   *FOESTER*   *ROTHE*
FREDERIKSEN   *H. L. ARNESEN*   *BAHNEBERG*

Filed By: CARL REIMERS

As the two Royal Government Councillors, Kunzen and Petersen, according to my ideas, could just as well have been in charge of the Government with full powers, notwithstanding that the Governor-General was sick, and there were even contradictory reports to the correctness of that., I, for my part, protested against acknowledging this new Government until I was certain as to how it had originated.

At half past four o'clock p.m. the men that had marched out in the morning returned with several of the leaders of the rising, upon which I again handed over the Fort to its Commander. Although the military which had returned had not met with any opposition on their march, and the negroes on many estates had shown that they wished for peace and order, there were yet many of them who sought to excite the better part of the population. For this reason, and in view of the necessity for action, Vice-Stadthauptmand F. v Scholten, Major Gyllich, Capt. v Castonier, Police Master Ogaard, Lawyer Sarauw and I were unanimous in publishing the following:

"As the Authorities here have received no answer from His Excellency the Governor-General to the Reports forwarded to him, nor any of the instructions requested, and having this day learned that on account of illness he is not in a condition to occupy himself with instructions, and as it is moreover necessary during the present negro rebellion in this jurisdiction to act immediately, we, the undersigned, as the highest authority in the place, have assembled to act until further."

Frederiksted, 6th July 1848.

F. SCHOLTEN   C. IRMINGER   CASTONIER
GYLLICH   OGAARD   SARAUW

We then made known:

"It is with the utmost satisfaction that the inhabitants of this jurisdiction have learned that order and obedience to the laws has commenced to be re-established, and as from most evidence the hope can be entertained that regularity and order will go hand in hand, it is hereby promulgated that any person or persons opposing the authorities, or in any other manner combining for illegal or violent purposes, will be dealt with as rioters and instantly shot. All peaceable and

well-disposed inhabitants are called upon to assist the authorities in quelling disorder and apprehending the rioters."

Frederiksted, 6ᵗʰ July 1848.

F. SCHOLTEN   C. IRMINGER   CASTONIER

GYLLICH   OGAARD   SARAUW

As many of the refugees on board the vessels were still in dread of the rioting negroes, and as there was some reason to suppose that in their fear they would remove from the island, in order to prevent them doing so, I forbade all ferrying with boats, from nine o'clock in the evening till four o'clock in the morning, which times were made known by a cannon shot from the brig.

On the 7ᵗʰ, the military again marched out in different directions. This had a good effect upon the negroes, and the roads became once more safe to traffic. In the Fort there were about one hundred rioters, of which the greater part had been brought in by the friendly negroes from the estates. A portion of the prisoners were taken on board the brig, and some distributed among the merchant vessels. In the meantime, an order was issued to all parties concerned that they should within three days deliver up all stolen goods and arms, as everyone, who after that time was found in possession of such, would be punished to the utmost extent of the law.

On the 8ᵗʰ, several carriages passed between Bassin and West End. Everything was quiet and safe on the road. Refugees from the vessels returned on shore to take up their residence in town. Sugar was brought in from several estates for shipment, and as everything now promised to go on smoothly, we, who had assembled as the highest authority in this place, handed over the charge of affairs to the Commander of the Fort and the Police Master.

At noon, 220-men auxiliary troops arrived in Frederiksted; 360 were already in Christiansted. The Governor-General had asked for this assistance from Porto Rico. As an instance of General Prim's[6] customary activity, it should be mentioned that this fine body of men, 580 all told, with cannon and 30,000 cartridges were got ready and put to sea five hours after he had received the letter from the Governor-General. This prompt action and the fact that the insurrection had been repressed in the eastern and western parts of the

---

6   **Then Captain-General of Porto Rico [today Puerto Rico].**

island, contributed much to allay the fears of the inhabitants, and to inspire confidence.

On the 9th, Chamberlain Oxholm came to West End and took over the Governor-General's affairs. In the meantime, the country was quiet, and the negroes had returned to work on a few of the estates. By this time several of the rioters had been tried by court-martial and shot.

From the reports, it will be seen that Kammerjunker Rothe was sent as a sort of "commissioner" to Frederiksted, in order to proclaim the new Government established in Bassin. As I had already agreed with Captain v Castonier to take over the command of the Fort with my men, while he undertook a march into the country with the military, I protested against subjecting myself to this Government because:

1. *I assumed after the account that Lieutenant Franck had given me, that the General v Scholten was not so sick but that he could have signed an order to me.*

2. *There were in the new Government several names almost unknown to me.*

3. *Kammerjunker Rothe did not produce anything in writing, either from General v Scholten, the existing Governor, or the other two Government Councillors, Kunzen and Petersen, concerning this newly appointed Government Commission.*

I, therefore, considered it my duty not to submit myself blindly to the command of this Commission, especially as the report said that the Governor-General had been deposed. When Captain Castonier returned in the afternoon, I informed him of my protest. He fully concurred with my views. Other authorities in Frederiksted followed our example, and although Vice-Stadthauptmand, Chamberlain F. v Scholten hesitated, he still signed the measures we took to restore order and quiet.

On the 12th July, I dispatched my report from West End to St. Thomas to leave by the packet for Europe. It bears that day's date. Written during the actual occurrence of the riots, it contains my view respecting the events as they then appeared to me. I have seen no reason to change them. I never imagined that General v Scholten would leave the island, which, as is known, happened immediately after; consequently, my report arrived home with the same packet on which he took passage.

On the 24th July, I left West End to be on hand to assist in St. Thomas. The 6th September I received orders to come with the "*Ørnen*" to Bassin as quickly as possible, as riots had occurred and it was not desirable, expect absolutely necessary, to use the Spaniards. The Fort in Bassin was now reinforced by men from the "*Ørnen*" because, as is known, the Government had given way to the Brand Corps and discharged the energetic Police-Master Friderichsen.

INTERIOR - CHRISTIANSVAERN FORT

Hans Kongelige Majestæts

til Danmark, de Venders og Gothers, Hertug til Slesvig, Holsteen, Stormarn, Ditmarsken

Lauenborg og Oldenborg

Bestalter

Excellence, Generalmajor, Kammerherre, Storkors af Dannebroge og Dannebrogsmand, Storkors af Isabella den Catholskes Orden, Storofficeer af Æreslegionen, Commandeur af Guelphe Ordenen, Ridder af Ordenen du merite militaire, General Gouverneur over de danske vestindiske Öer,

JEG

Peter Carl Frederik v. Scholten

Giör vitterligt :	*Maketh known :*
1.	**1.**
Alle Ufrie paa de danske vestindiske Öer ere fra Dags Dato frigivne.	All Unfree in the danish westindia Islands are from to-day emancipated.
2.	**2.**
Negerne paa Plantagerne beholde i 3 Maaneder fra Dato Brugen af de Huse og Provisionsgrunde, hvoraf de nu ere i Besiddelse.	The Estate Negroes retain for three months from date the use of the houses and provisiongrounds, of which they have hitherto been possessed.
3.	**3.**
Arbeide betales for Fremtiden efter Overeenskomst, hvorimod Allowance ophörer.	Labour is in future to be paid for by agreement, but allowance is to cease.
4.	**4.**
Underholdningen af Gamle og Svage, som ere ude af Stand til at arbeide, afholdes indtil nærmere Bestemmelse af deres forrige Eiere.	The maintainance of old and infirm, who are not able to work, is until farther determination to be furnished by the late owners.

Givet under General Gouvernementets Segl og min Haand.

General Gouvernementet over de danske vestindiske Öer, St. Croix den 3die Juli 1848.

[L. S.]   **P. v. Scholten.**

The printed Proclamation from 1848, where Governor-General Peter von Scholten announced the abolition of slavery in the Danish West Indies.

CHAPTER V

GENERAL BUDDHOE'S FAMILY

THIS CHAPTER CONTAINS A PHOTOGRAPH OF GENERAL BUDDHOE, HIS birth/baptismal certificate showing he was born on St. Croix on the 19th day of March, 1820 on Plantation La Grange. He was a Lutheran. At the time of Emancipation he was 28 years old.

There is also information about his mother (Maria Rosina) and his two sisters (Mathilda and Leah "Sanchy" Petrus). Note that his sister Leah named one of her sons for her brother, John Gottlieb, who would later play a major role in the Fireburn of 1878. Leah was also listed in a police report from Frederiks Fort for "rudely talking back to" a Danish fort official when she attempted to visit her brother General Buddhoe at the fort after his arrest. She was only 15 years old at the time.

There are three very interesting finds here:

1. A man named "John Gottlieb," of Plantation Estate La Grange, born in 1799 that could possibly be Buddhoe's father;
2. A lady by the name of "Maryan Gottlieb," born in 1794, who is possibly his aunt (his father's sister); and
3. General Buddhoe's mother, Maria Rosina's, marriage to Anthony George at the Moravian Church, Frederiksted on February 22, 1846. Maria Rosina was 49 years old at the time of the Emancipation; lived at Plantation La Grange and died on November 4, 1877 at the age of 78.

THE HONORABLE JOHN "GENERAL BUDDHOE" GOTTLIEB
(also spelled "GOTLIFF," "GOTLIEB" and "GUTLIFF.")

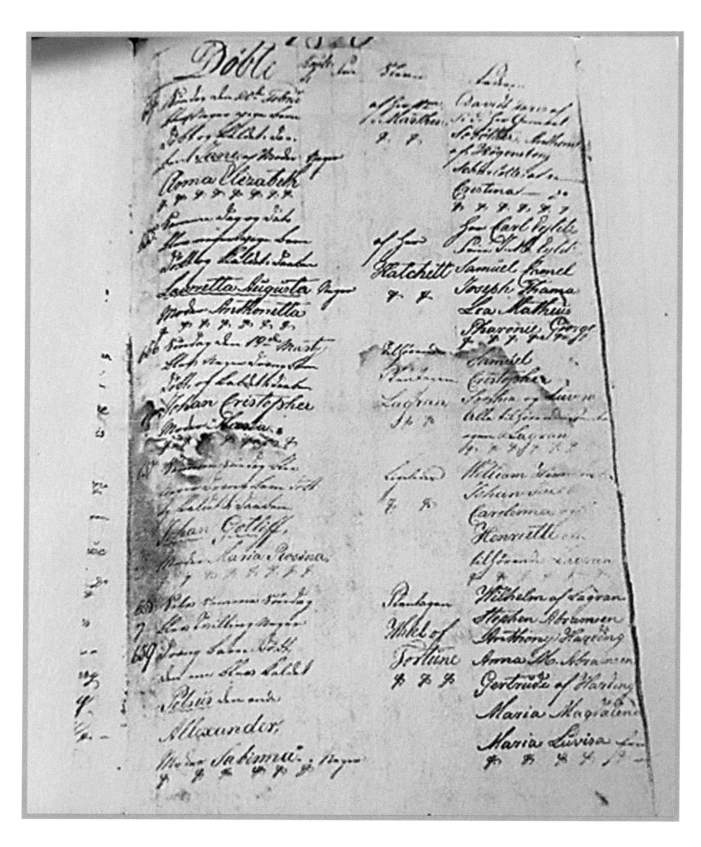

**GENERAL BUDDHOE'S BIRTH/BAPTISMAL CERTIFICATE FROM
HOLY TRINITY LUTHERAN CHURCH, FREDERIKSTED.**

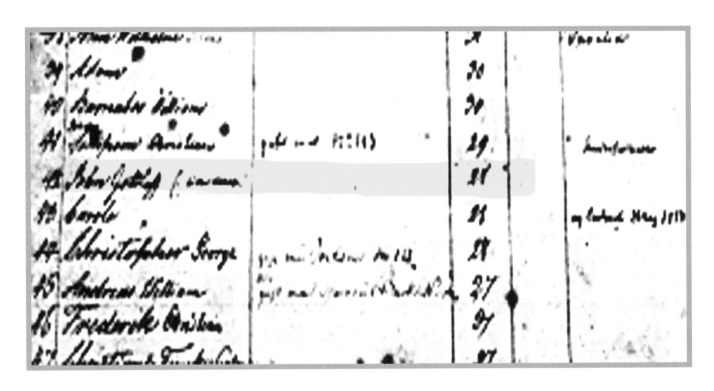

GENERAL BUDDHOE (AGE 28) ON AN INVENTORY OF SLAVES FROM PLANTATION LA GRANGE IN 1848.

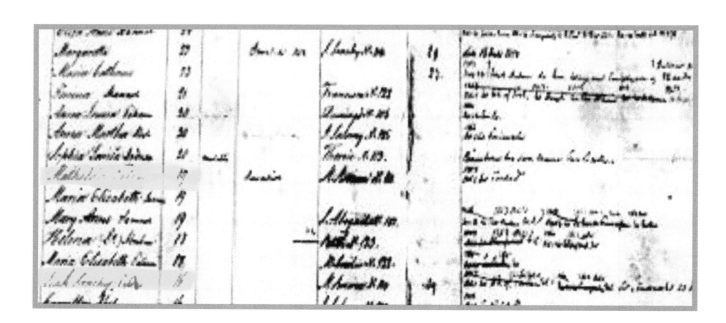

GENERAL BUDDHOE'S SISTERS (MATHILDA PETRUS, AGE 19 AND LEAH
"SANCHY" PETRUS, AGE 15) AT THE TIME OF THE EMANCIPATION.

MATHILDA WAS BORN IN 1829. LEAH WAS BORN IN 1832 AND DIED
FEBRUARY 23, 1871. MATHILDA IS LISTED AS "INVALID" MEANING SHE WAS
UNABLE TO WORK. BOTH WERE BORN ON PLANTATION LA GRANGE.

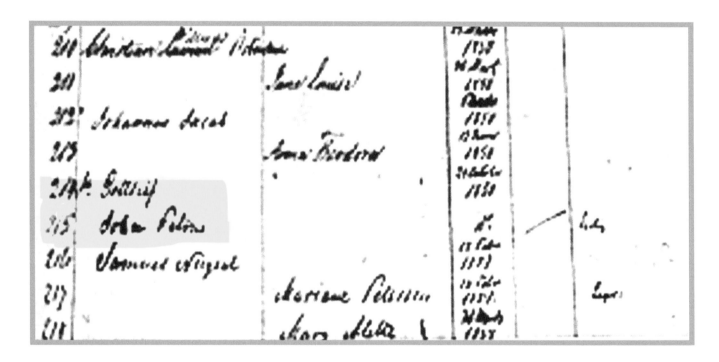

GENERAL BUDDHOE'S SISTER, LEAH "SANCHY" PETRUS NAMED HER SON FOR GENERAL BUDDHOE (JOHN GOTTLIEB) BORN OCTOBER 24, 1850. SHE HAD A TOTAL OF THREE SONS (AARON, BORN JULY 25, 1849; JOHN, BORN 1850 AND ANTHONY ISAAC, BORN OCTOBER 24, 1852. AARON DIED AS AN INFANT FIVE DAYS AFTER HIS BIRTH ON JULY 30, 1849.

GENERAL BUDDHOE'S SISTER, MATHILDA, ALSO HAD A SON BY THE NAME OF CHRISTIAN JOSEPH WILLIAMS, BORN SEPTEMBER 11, 1857 IN FREDERIKSTED (WHO WOULD ALSO PLAY A MAJOR ROLE IN THE FIREBURN OF 1878).

GENERAL BUDDHOE'S MOTHER, MARIA ROSINA, WAS 49 YEARS OLD IN 1848; LIVED ON PLANTATION LA GRANGE AND DIED OF A SUDDEN HEMORRHAGE ON NOVEMBER 4, 1877 AT THE AGE OF 78.

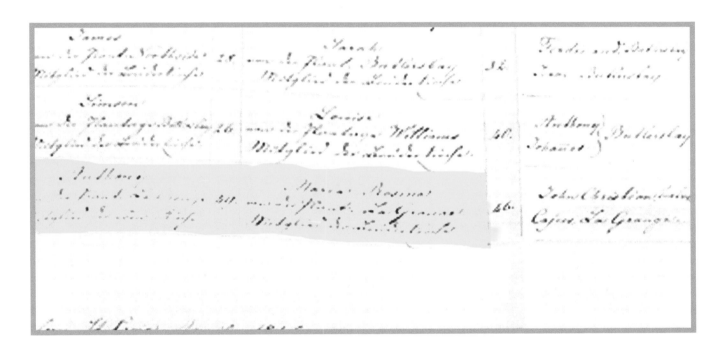

THE MARRIAGE OF GENERAL BUDDHOE'S MOTHER, MARIA ROSINA TO ANTHONY GEORGE, BOTH OF PLANTATION LA GRANGE, AT THE FREDERIKSTED MORAVIAN CHURCH ON FEBRUARY 22, 1846. HE WAS 49 YEARS OLD; SHE WAS 46.

A GENTLEMAN NAMED "JOHN GOTTLIEB" BORN 1799 ON PLANTATION LA GRANGE LISTED AS A GODFATHER FOR "BABY WILHELM." THIS IS POSSIBLY GENERAL BUDDHOE'S FATHER.

A POSSIBLE PATERNAL AUNT OF GENERAL BUDDHOE,
MARYAN GOTTLIEB, BORN 1794 IN FREDERIKSTED.

A POLICE REPORT REFLECTING THE ARREST OF GENERAL BUDDHOE'S SISTER (LEAH "SANCHY" PETRUS) OF PLANTATION LA GRANGE FOR *"RUDELY TALKING BACK TO"* A DANISH OFFICIAL AT THE FORT, WHERE SHE HAD GONE TO TRY TO VISIT HER BROTHER AFTER HIS ARREST. SHE WAS ONLY 15 YEARS OLD AT THE TIME.

CHAPTER VI

ADMIRAL MARTIN KING'S FAMILY

THIS CHAPTER CONTAINS A PHOTOGRAPH OF ADMIRAL MARTIN KING (taken from the 150th Emancipation Commemoration Booklet).

It also contains the 1860 Census listing Martin King at 43 years old. According to the Census, King was born in 1817 and would have been 31 years old at the time of Emancipation. He is also listed as a Roman Catholic. He was also married to a woman by the name of Severina of Plantation St. Georges, who died in October of 1848. Thus far, I have not been able to find his death records.

After his two-year imprisonment, he seemed to have returned to Plantation Bog of Allen. The 1857 Census list him living with his mother at Plantation Allandale, as she was no longer able to work. However, he would later move to Plantation Prosperity and is listed as a "1st Class Cartman" on that plantation.

His mother, Hannah [*only her first name is listed*] is listed as a Cook; also as a Roman Catholic; has two children and was born in 1798. She is included on the Censuses of 1846, 1850, 1857 and 1860 living at Plantation Bog of Allen.

James King is listed in a translation of a police report as Martin King's father who "relaxed" when Martin King was seized and arrested. James King was born in 1795; is listed as a Saddler and died on June 16, 1866 of a fever at the age of 71.

THE HONORABLE ADMIRAL MARTIN KING

REGISTER
of Unfree living in the Country in

For the Estate called *Bog of Allen* situated in *Princes* Quarter, No. *10*, belonging to *Mrs. Dewhurst* consisting of *150* Acres of Land, of which *97* Acres in Sugar cultivation, *53* Acres in provision and pasture Land, and ~~ Acres entirely useless.

LIVING ON THE ESTATE.	Males.	Females.	Total.	Where born.	Age, the remaining year	and when Baptized.	Married, Unmarried Widow	Mother of how many	An House Servant.	Blacksmith.	Mason.	Carpenter.	Cooper.	belonging to the big	belonging to the small	Incapable of working.	Moral Character.	or by the Governor-General Resolution and how & when punished.
Thomas	1	~	~	St brive	31	Catholick 1815	unm	~	~	~	~	~	~	1	~	~	Good	never
Martin	1	~	~	ditto	29	ditto 1817	do	~	~	~	~	~	1	cartman			good	never
Mike	1	~	~	ditto	33	English 1813	do	~	1	~	~	~	~	~			good	never
Agness	~	1	~	St croix	35	English	do	1	~	~	~	~	~	1	~		good	never
Ann Mary	~	1	~	ditto	33	Catholick 1813	do	1	~	~	~	~	~	1	~		good	never
Emma	~	1	~	Africa	26	Maravian 1820	do	~	~	~	~	~	~	1	~		gad	never
Frederica	~	1	~	St croix	31	Catholick 1815	do	4	~	~	~	~	~	1	~		midling	never
Joan	~	1	~	ditto	21	English 1825	do	~	~	~	~	~	~	1	~		Ditto	never
Hanna	~	1	~	ditto	47	Catholick 1799	do	2	~	~	~	~	~	1	~		good	never
Jennet	~	1	~	Africa	25	Maravian 1831	do	1	~	~	~	~	~	1	~		good	never
Jinny	~	1	~	St croix	34	Catholick 1812	do	3	~	~	~	~	~	1	~		good	never
Isabella	~	1	~	ditto	71	Maravian	do	4	~	~	~	~	~	1	~		good	never

A CENSUS LISTING OF PLANTATION BOG OF ALLEN IN 1846 SHOWING MARTIN KING AT AGE 29, BORN IN 1817, HENCE AGE 31 AT THE TIME OF THE EMANCIPATION. IT ALSO LIST HIM AS A 1ST CLASS CARTMAN AND AS A CATHOLIC OF *GOOD MORAL CHARACTER.*

THE SAME CENSUS LIST HIS MOTHER (HANNAH) AT 47 YEARS OLD; BORN IN 1799 AND AS HAVING TWO CHILDREN.

NOTE THAT THE REGISTER LIST ESTATE BOG OF ALLEN IN 1846 CONSISTING OF 150 ACRES, OF WHICH 97 WERE IN SUGAR CULTIVATION; THE REMAINING 53 ACRES IN PROVISION AND PASTURE LAND WITH 0 ACRES BEING ENTIRELY USELESS, AND IT WAS OWNED BY MRS. ELIZABETH DEWHURST.

No. 2 REGISTER of Unfree living in the Country in St. Croix.

For the Estate called *St. Georges & Hope* situated in *Princes* Quarter, No. _____ , belonging to *His Majesty the King* consisting of *450* Acres of Land, of which *280* Acres in Sugar cultivation, *170* Acres in provision and pasture Land, and _____ Acres entirely useless.

Names of all the Unfree living on the Estate.				Where born.	Age, the running year included.	Religion and when Baptised.	Married, Unmarried, Widower, or Widow.	Mother of how many children a live.	House Servant.			belonging to the big gang.	belonging to the small gang.	Situation of working	Moral Character.	If ever as criminals punished by Judgement or by the Governor General's Resolution and how & when punished.

Harriett	1		.		31	Catholic Church 11 Febry 1811.	.	4.			1		.		✓	,
Ellen /Big	1	.			27	Catholic Church 14 June 1811.	.	2.			1		.		✓	.
Cally	1		.		29	Catholic Church 11 Septr 1815.	.				1		.		✓	.
Cecilia	1		.		29	Catholic Church 3 Augt 1812.	.	1			1		.		✓	.
Amalia /St. G	1		.		33	Lutheran Ch. 10 March 1813.	.				1		.		✓	.
Catharine	1		.		31	Lutheran Ch. 15 January 1809.	.				1		.		✓	.
Eva Maria	1		.		26	Lutheran Church 3 Octr 1811.	.				1		.		✓	.
Ellen /L	1		.		23	Lutheran Ch. 30 Septr 1816.	.	1			1		.		✓	.
Sue	1		.		29	Catholic Ch. 28 February 1814	.				1		.		✓	.
Severina	1		.		25	Catholic Church 1 May 1813.	.				1		.		✓	.
Catharine	1		.		23	Catholic Church 18 Augt 1817.	.				1		.		✓	.
Leah	1		.		21	Lutheran Church 2nd April 1819	.				1		.		✓	.
Silby	1		.		19	Catholic Church 7 July 1821.	.				1		.		✓	.

THIS 1841 CENSUS LIST MARTIN KING'S WIFE (SEVERINA) OF PLANTATION ST. GEORGES, AT 25 YEARS OLD, BORN AUGUST 18, 1817, AND ALSO BAPTIZED AS A ROMAN CATHOLIC.

Date of Death	Where Entered	Name of Deceased	When and When Baptized	If Married	Age	Formerly belong to	Disease
05 Oct 1st	West End	Augustine	West End	No	70	The King	Old Age
06 Oct 3	St Georges	Severina	West End	No	22	St Georges	Consumption
07 Oct 7	Poor Friends	Patrick	West End	No	50	Poor Friends	Fever
08 Oct 14	Fountain	Daniel	West End	No	27	Fountain	Consumption
09 Oct 14	Paradise	Bridget	West End	No	24	Paradise	Bowels
10 Oct 15	Fountain	Mary	West End	No	80	Fountain	Old Age

ST. PATRICK'S CATHOLIC CHURCH DEATH RECORDS OF
FOURTH QUARTER 1848 SHOWING SEVERINA OF PLANTATION
ST. GEORGES DIED JUST A SHORT 3 MONTHS (TO THE DAY)
AFTER EMANCIPATION ON OCTOBER 3, 1848 OF "CONSUMPTION."

~~~~~

THE AGE LISTED FOR HER ON THE CENSUS IS OBVIOUSLY A MISTAKE.
SHE WAS BORN ON AUGUST 18, 1817, SO IT SHOULD
HAVE SAID AGE "32" INSTEAD OF "22."

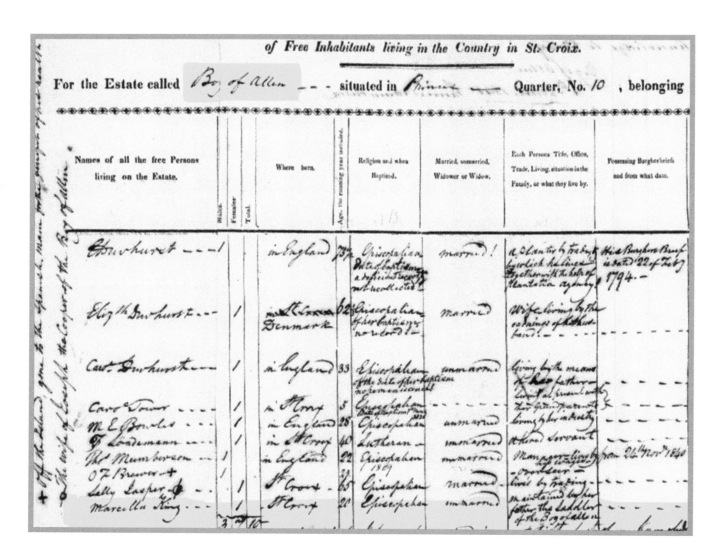

MERCELLA KING (MARTIN KING'S SISTER) IS LISTED ON THIS 1841 CENSUS AT PLANTATION BOG OF ALLEN. SHE IS 20 YEARS OLD AT THAT TIME. IT SAYS *"MAINTENANCE BY HER FATHER, THE SADDLER OF THE BOG OF ALLEN."*

MERCELLA WAS NAMED FOR HER AUNT (HER FATHER'S SISTER) WHO WAS BORN IN 1794.

THE 1860 CENSUS LIST MARTIN KING AT AGE 43 IN 1860 AND
AS A 1ST CLASS CARTMAN ON PLANTATION PROSPERITY.

For the Estate called *Bog of allen* situated in *Prince* Quarter, No. , belonging to *Mrs Dewhurst*

NAMES OF ALL THE FREE PERSONS LIVING ON THE ESTATE.	Males.	Females.	Total.	Where born.	Ages, their running your last noted.	Religion and when Baptized.	Married, unmarried, Widower or Widow.	Each Person Title, Office, Trade, Living, situation in the Family, or what they live by.	Possessing Burgherbrieb, and from what date.	In which Militia Corps doing duty and in what capacity.
Mrs. Dewhurst	..	1	..	Copenhagen	53	Baptized in the Episcopal Ch. Baptized	Widow	by his Revenues		.
Miss Jane Caroline Dewhurst	..	1	..	London	36	ditto	unmarried	Supported by her Mother Mrs Dewhurst		
Catherine Bogle	..	1	..	St. Croix	28	ditto	unmarried	Ladies Maid	..	..
Edward Murphy	1	..	..	Ireland	28	Baptized in the Catholick Church 18th April 1818	unmarried	Manager	Having a Burgherbrieb from 18th July 1846	8 Division W. E. Comps
Charles Carrigan	1	..	..	Ditto	21	Catholick Church 16th May 1825	Ditto	overseer	None	Ditto
James King	1	..	..	St. Croix	50	Episcopal Ch. Baptized	ditto	Sadler	..	Brand Corps
Missila King	..	1	..	ditto	25	ditto	ditto	Sarnett S	..	
Sally Nelson	..	1	..	ditto	65	ditto	married	Supported by Son	..	..
Caroline White	..	1	..	ditto	55	ditto	ditto	ditto by Mr		

THE 1846 CENSUS LIST JAMES KING ON PLANTATION BOG OF ALLEN, AGE 50, AND AS A SADDLER IN THE BRAND CORPS. IT ALSO LISTS HIS DAUGHTER MISSILA[MERCELLA] AS A SEAMSTRESS AT AGE 25.

JAMES WAS BAPTIZED IN THE EPISCOPAL CHURCH.

The 1866 Frederiksted death record table showing columns: Date of Burial, Still Born, Name and Age of Deceased and whether Married &c. (Males / Females), Occupation, Residence.

Date of Burial	Still Born	Males		Females		Occupation	Residence
1866							
44 April 19				Mary Ann Jordan	83 Months	None	
45 · 24		Mark Moore	4 1/2			None	
46 · 25				Elizabeth Thomas	28	Labour	
47 · 26		Adam John	49			Labour	
48 · 29		Joseph Richards	9 days			None	
49 May 1				Nancy Mackle	18	Domestic	
50 · 2		James Love	12			Labour	
51 · 6		Mary Jacobson	48			Labour	
52 · 7		Abram Williams	38			Labour	
53 · 8				Elizabeth Stevens	3 Months	None	
54 · 9				Margaret	7 Months	None	
55 · 10		William Henry Richardson	12			Labour	
56 · 11		Henry Thomas Austin	22			Labour	
57 · 17				Victoria Jane Thompson	4 Months	None	
58 · 24				Lucia James	9 days	None	
59 · 26					7 Months	None	
60 · 26		Charles Williams				Domestic	
61 · 30		Frank Richard				Labour	
62 · 30				Charlotte Roberts	8 Days	None	
63 · 31		Wm Austin Ventura	5 Mths			None	
64 June 7		Isaac	70			Labour	
65 · 7				Salethal Payne	6 Days	None	
66 · 12		Adam Logan	80			Healer	
67 · 12		William Folk	40			Labour	
68 · 13				Marietta Williams	1	None	
69 · 13		William Burdsons	2			None	
70 · 14				Matthew	80	Domestic	
71 · 16		James King	71			Saddler	
72 · 18				Sarah Jane	2 Months	None	
73 · 20				Barbara	1	None	
74 · 21		Isaac	29			Labour	
75 · 21				Mary Ann	4	None	
76 · 22				Rachel		Labour	
77 · 25				Mary Carroll	2	None	
78 · 27		Richard Matthew	13			Blacksmith	
79 · 24		Peter Andrew				Domestic	
80 · 30		Johannes Williams	10 Mths			None	
81 July 4		Samuel Wilkes				None	
82 · 10				Nancy	2 Months	None	
83 · 11				Sophia George	26		
84 · 14		William James					
85 · 15		Beale	60			Cooper	
86 · 20				Mary George		None	

THE 1866 FREDERIKSTED DEATH RECORDS SHOWS JAMES KING, A SADDLER, DIED ON JUNE 16, 1866 AT AGE 71 FROM A FEVER.

Names of all persons living on the Estate.	Males.	Females.	Total.	Where born.	Age, the running year included.	Religion and when baptised.	Married, Unmarried.	Widower, Widow.	Each Person Title, Office, Trade, Living, and relative state in the family.	Persons infected with the leprosy.
Brought Over	31	19	50							
Johny	1			Saint Croix	31	Catholic bapt. some year	Unmarried	Do	1st Class Labour	
Joan		1		Ditto	26	English	Do	Do	Do Do	Do
Anna Martha		1		Ditto	23	Catholic	Do	Do	1. Do Do	Do
Georgianna		1		Ditto	21	English	Do	Do	1. Do Do	Do
Ellen		1		Ditto	20	Ditto	Do	Do	2nd Do Do	Do
Rosaline		1		Ditto	21	Ditto	Do	Do	1st Do Do	Do
Nelly		1		Ditto	16	Catholic	Do	Do	2nd Class Do	
Mary Eliza		1		Ditto	15	English	Do	Do	2.. Do Do	Do
Belinda		1		Ditto	13	Catholic	Do	Do	2.. Do Do	
Mary Jane		1		Ditto	13	Ditto	Do	Do	2.. Do Do	
Christopher	1			Ditto	10	Ditto	Do	Do	not at work as yet	
John Fair	1			Ditto	6	Ditto	Do	Do	Do Do Do	
Cathrine		1		Ditto	7	Ditto	Do	Do	Do Do Do	
Caroline		1		Ditto	5	English	Do	Do	Do Do Do	
Sarah		1		Ditto	1	Do	Do	Do	Do Do Do	
Victoria		1		Ditto	2	Do	Do	Do	Do Do Do	
Wm Augustus	1			Ditto	3	Do	Do	Do	Do Do Do	
Allick	1			Ditto	1	Do	Do	Do		
Madelaine		1		Ditto	45	Catholic	Do	Do	2nd Class Labour	
Wm George	1			Ditto	22	English	Do	Do	Cooper & Mason	
Cow George	1			Ditto	25	Catholic	Do	Do	Watchman	
Bella		1		Ditto	25	Do	Do	Do	1st Class Labour	
Esther		1		Ditto	4?	Ditto	Do	Do	1. Do Do	
Frederick	1			Ditto	4?	Ditto	Do	Do	Do Do Do	
Jane		1		Ditto	6	English	Do	Do	Not at work as yet	
Wm Frederick	1			Ditto	1	Catholic	Do	Do	Ditto Do	
David	1			Ditto	1	English	Do	Do	Ditto Do	
Hannah		1		Ditto	52	Catholic	Do	Do	Cook	
Jinetta		1		Ditto	50	Moravian	Do	Do	1st Class Labour	
Isabella		1		Ditto	59	Ditto	Do	Married	Allowed to reside	
Jinny		1		Ditto	30	Catholic	Do	Ditto	1st Class Labour	
Kitty		1		Ditto	40	English	Do	Unmarried	1.. Do Do	
Christian Matthew Simbra	1			Ditto	1	Catholic	Do	Do	Not at work	
Sally Gosper		1		Ditto	74	English	Do	Married	Allowed to reside	
Rebeca Williams		1		Ditto	59	Catholic	Do	Unmarried	Do .. Do	
Wm Morrison	1			Ditto	27	English	Do	Do	Do Taylor	
Jossy		1		Africa	69	Catholic bap 1806	Do	Do	Superanuated	
Catherine Eccles		1		Saint Croix	24	Do	Do	Do	House Keeper	
Alexander Knott	1			Ireland	29	English	Do	Do	Manager	
Aley. Knott Jun.	1			Saint Croix	6	Catholic	Do	Do	Living with his Father	
	44	46	90							

How many families on the Estate. 12 large families

5 married families

St Croix 17th May 1850

A Knott

ADMIRAL MARTIN KING'S MOTHER (HANNAH) IS LISTED ON THIS
1850 CENSUS AS A COOK ON PLANTATION BOG OF ALLEN.

PAGE 408 - (Dated July 22, 1848)

DANISH TEXT: James King, relaxeret, den [?] hans son, Martin King: i Dag er bleven paagrebend af Driverent Isaac af Pl. Paradise, og arresterent I Fortet.

ENGLISH TRANSLATION: James King relaxed, that [?] his son, Martin King, today was seized by Isaac the driver of Plantation Paradise and arrested in the Fort.

Aarhus University
School of Culture and Society
Department of Archaeology and Heritage Studies
Postdoc – Enduring Materialities of Colonialism
"As scholars tasked with the important work of recounting the lived experiences of the oppressed and marginalized, we ought to "Pray for the Living and Fight LIKE HELL FOR THE DEAD." – Peter H. Wood

CHAPTER VII

BUDDHOE'S EMANCIPATION DAY ACTIVITIES

THIS CHAPTER CONTAINS A PHOTOGRAPH OF GENERAL BUDDHOE JUST before boarding the *Brig-of-war Ørnen* while imprisoned at Christiansvaern Fort. This photograph was taken from the 150th Emancipation Commemoration Booklet.

This Chapter also contains a very interesting letter from the 100th Centennial Emancipation Day Celebration Booklet written by R. H. Amphlett Leader entitled "Mensis Mirabilis," where Leader declares ***"...no white person, with the exception of Governor-General von Scholten himself, knew or even suspected, what was brewing."*** Leader concluded that General Buddhoe and Peter von Scholten worked collaboratively to effectuate the Emancipation.

This conclusion was also drawn by Royal Councillor von Petersen in his writing where he declared: ***"Many are of the opinion that Governor-General von Scholten knew in advance that the rebellion would take place and could have prevented it by early precautions..."*** *(Page 145)*. Further, this same conclusion was also drawn and/or suggested by Thorkild Hansen *"Islands of Slaves" (Page 420)*; John P. Knox *"A Historical Account of St. Thomas, W.I.," (Page 119)* ; Charles E. Taylor *"Leaflets from the Danish West Indies" (Page 130)* and Neville Hall *"Slave Society in the Danish West Indies" (Page 204)*.

**GENERAL BUDDHOE AWAITING DEPORTATION AT
CHRISTIANSVAERN FORT – DECEMBER 1848.**

Mensis Mirabilis
An Historical Sketch of the Virgin Islands

By R. H. AMPHLETT LEADER, LL.B.
Noted Writer & Lecturer

PEAKING ABOUT freedom and liberty, is there a lucky month? If there is, then July is that month. Even a cursory examination of history will show that more countries and peoples have severed the chains of political and physical slavery during the month of July than during any other month.

The United States of America declared its independence on July 4, 1776; the French people stormed and destroyed the Bastile on July 14, 1789; it was during the month of July, 1801, while Toussaint L'Ouverture was master of the whole island of Santo Domingo that the Constitution of Santo Domingo which provided for free trade—the first enactment of its kind in the history of the world—became law; Venezuela obtained its independence from Spain on July 5, 1811, Argentina on July 9, 1816; Peru on July 28, 1821; Belgium came from under the dominance of Holland on July 21, 1831; and it was on July 3, 1848, at eight o'clock in the morning that over 2,500 slaves from the northside estates and upwards of 4,000 from the southside and centerline estates marched to Frederiksted, assembled before the fort and demanded their freedom immediately. The insurrection was on. The demand for freedom grew louder and louder until Governor-General von Scholten arrived from Christiansted and from the battery of the fort proclaimed freedom of the slaves. Certainly, when we are thinking or speaking of the freedom and liberty of countries and peoples we must consider that the month of July is MENSIS MIRABILIS—month of wonders.

The chief actors in the drama of our MENSIS MIRABILIS were "General Bordeaux" (Buddhoe), his able "Lieutenant" Martin King, Governor-General Peter C. F. von Scholten, Governor of St. Croix and Chamberlain Frederik von Scholten, brother of the Governor. It has been said that neither the white population nor the goodly number of free Negroes, who were intelligent and in many instances well educated, knew anything of the planning of Bordeaux. This is largely correct. No white person, with the exception of Governor-General von Scholten himself, knew, or even suspected, what was brewing. However, there is evidence that four, and possibly five, educated colored men, three of whom were members of the Governor-General's favorite Jaeger Corps, knew of and assisted in the "movement", and were constantly in touch with Bordeaux.

Bordeaux, allegedly the son of an African Chieftain, must have been a born leader of men. Young, he was 36 years at the time of the insurrection, he was wise beyond his years. The "movement" for freedom must have taken months of preparation and arrangement. The slaves on each and every estate had to be contacted. The person who made these contacts was Bordeaux for it was he whom his fellow slaves loved and respected. His residence was at Estate La Grange, but fortunately, because of his knowledge of certain things he was "lent out" or "hired out", throughout the island. So well planned was the "movement" that the entire slave population—those who were to march on Frederiksted, and those who were to remain on the estates—were notified of the crucial moment by drum telegraphy.

But no history tells of William Peebles, barely 18 years and the youngest member of the Jaeger Corps, who was in the march from Christiansted to Frederiksted with five minutes rest at Kingshill, who later was on guard at Government House and challenged "Who goes there?" receiving the reply "Your Governor" as von Scholten opened his cloak revealing his insignia of office and proceeded on his way to board the vessel which was lying in the water bordering the Christiansted Utilities Lumber Shed. I wonder if Gideon Peebles, the grandson of William Peebles, know these facts!

Thus the Virgin Islands celebrate the Centennial of its MENSIS MIRABILIS!

The Emancipation Proclamation

1. All Unfree in the Danish West India Islands are from today emancipated.

2. The estate Negroes retain for three months from date the use of the houses and provision grounds of which they have hitherto been possessed.

3. Labor is in future to be paid for by agreement, but allowance to cease.

4. The maintenance of old and infirm, who are not able to work is until further determination to be furnished by the late owners.

Givet under General Gouvernementets Segl og min Haand.

General Gouvernementet over de danske vestindiske Oer den 2die Julii 1848.

P. v. SCHOLTEN.

THIS SUBMISSION WAS WRITTEN BY R.H. AMPHLETT LEADER AND APPEARED IN THE 100TH CENTENNIAL ANNIVERSARY BOOKLET IN 1948.

DANISH TEXT: Gotlieb Boudeau: Fremstod og modtog sit Pas til Tortola. Han er fodt paa St. Croix, er 30 Aar gammel, hoi 5 fod 6 ½ Tommer dansk Maal, er middelmaadig af Positur, har sorte One og sort krollet haar, men ingen andre Maerker.

ENGLISH TRANSLATION: Gotlieb Boudeau, appeared and received his passport for Tortola. He was born on St. Croix, is about 30 years old, is 5 feet 6 ½ Danish inches tall, is of medium build, has black eyes and black curly hair, but no other marks.

Aarhus University
School of Culture and Society
Department of Archaeology and Heritage Studies
Postdoc – Enduring Materialities of Colonialism
"As scholars tasked with the important work of recounting the lived experiences of the oppressed and marginalized, we ought to "Pray for the Living and Fight LIKE HELL FOR THE DEAD." – Peter H. Wood

DANISH TEXT: Gotlieb Bourdeau: modte paa Politikammeret med en Skrivelse fra Major v. Gyllich, hvormed det ham tilstillede Reisepas retourneres da han horer at flere Plantere onsker at han skal forblive her.

Gotlieb Bourdeau: Modtaget Skrivelse fra G. Gouverneuren om at Gottlieb Bourdeau ei maa meddeles Pas uden Gourvernementets Tilladelse, samt han han skall vaere tilstaede her i Byen naar G. Gouverneuren onsker at tale med ham.…

ENGLISH TRANSLATION: Gotlieb Bourdeau: appeared at the Police Chamber with a letter from Major v. Gyllich, by which the passport issued to him is returned as he hears that several planters want him to remain here.

Gotlieb Bourdeau: Received a letter from the Governor that Gotlieb Bourdeau must not be granted a passport without the Government's permission, and that he must be present here in the city when the Governor wishes to speak with him.…

Aarhus University
School of Culture and Society
Department of Archaeology and Heritage Studies
Postdoc – Enduring Materialities of Colonialism
"As scholars tasked with the important work of recounting the lived experiences of the oppressed and marginalized, we ought to "Pray for the Living and Fight LIKE HELL FOR THE DEAD." – Peter H. Wood

CHAPTER VIII

MARTIN KING'S EMANCIPATION DAY ACTIVITIES

THIS CHAPTER CONTAINS INFORMATION ON MARTIN KING'S Emancipation Day activities from deposition testimony given by Major Gyllich of his encounters with Admiral Martin King and some members of his "Fleet" on July 3, 1848, and shortly thereafter.

Major Gyllich gave a very comprehensive and detailed narrative to the court about his interactions with Admiral Martin King, even letting the court know that he included King in his entourage as they went from plantation to plantation to read the Proclamation. Also, Lieutenant Richard Beech's brief testimony is included.

Admiral Martin King and Major Gyllich (along with General Buddhoe and others) rode together to many mid-island plantations where Gyllich witnessed first-hand the great influence and respect that Admiral Martin King received from his comrades on the plantations they visited.

This testimony clearly demonstrates how Major Gyllich undoubtedly came to respect and indeed admire Admiral Martin King.

There's also a listing of Admiral Martin King's "Fleet" by name.

Major Gyllich

[Anno 1848 July 26th at nine o'clock in the morning, the examination was continued].

Major Gyllich appeared and explained that when he Tuesday 4th of this month went around the country to read aloud the Proclamation of the Emancipation, he arrived together with Mr. Lieutenant Beech and Mr. Robinson to the Plantation Slob. He believes it was at nearly two o'clock. In the entourage of the person questioned was also the negro Bordeaux from La Grange, who had exerted a great influence on the people on the northside, but who said expressly that he could not have done much down in the country.

As the person questioned came closer to Plantation Slob, there was a large crowd of people. When they had entered, Martin King came, riding on a white horse, coming close to the person questioned and shouted in a fierce and violent tone, holding a saber in front of himself in a threatening way: "What do you come for?" "Who did send you?" "What brought you here?"[7]

When the person questioned said that he came to read the Proclamation, Martin King answered that they did not want to hear anything, that blood had been shed in Christiansted although they (the negroes) had not killed any white man, that they wanted revenge, blood for blood, life for life. Some slaves had been shot, among others, a good man, whose entrails had rushed out of his body.

He was wild and furious to a great extent, but he made no attempt to attack the person questioned or his entourage. Talking to him for a long time in a calming way he became a little quieter and got off the horse. And as the person questioned and his entourage continued trying to calm him down, saying that if they thirsted for blood, they could take theirs, he suddenly changed his mind, fell to his knees and made the sign of the cross over his own head and cried out that "there should be peace now!"

The person questioned firmly declared -- which the previous part of his explanation also sufficiently suggests -- that Martin King spoke to him both in his own name and in the name of the crowd, and that his speech on no condition can be regarded as a warning but more as a threat, and there was for that moment no reason for thinking that such threats were directed against the person questioned and his entourage personally.

Also there cannot be the slightest doubt about Martin King's exercising of a great influence on the crowd, while he still was violent, and this influence was also obvious when he commanded peace, for all became quiet. Martin King ordered that the ringing of the bells and blowing on "shells" should stop, and it was stopped at once. The person questioned also thinks that he sent some persons out to various places to stop destruction, at least he was told so. And when the person questioned later said that he had heard that

---

[7]   "What...here" is in English in the manuscript.

there were riots at Blessing, Martin King answered that he should take it easy, everything would be fine.

After that, the person questioned rode with his entourage, accompanied by Martin King, to Plantation La Reine, where a lot of negroes had gathered, some of them armed with bayonets on sticks and other such weapons. They looked in general wild, but when Martin King rode up to them and proclaimed peace, they became quiet. However, there was one among them who shouted that he would not hear anything about peace, but Martin King set after him and slashed at him with his saber.

After that, they first rode to Plantation Glynn, and after that to Mon Bijou, at both places everything was quiet. After that they went to Mt. Pleasant (East) where the crowd already had destructed the farmhouse and was breaking up the "works." The negroes were extremely wild and restless, and although Martin King made all possible effort, making them quiet was most difficult and it looked as if Martin King did not have very much power or influence over them. Nothing happened at all that gave reason to assume that Martin King by the gathered crowd was regarded as a leader or commander.

From here the person questioned rode together with Martin King and the other companions to Jealousy where nothing remarkable was found. This was also the case at the next plantation, Plantation Castle, from where the person questioned with entourage via the Centerline went back to West End. By the side street that leads down to Plantation Bog of Allen, Martin King left them, saying that he would go home, as he was hungry and tired. At that time, it was most likely about six o'clock.

On the way to Slob, Bordeaux did not in any way talk about Martin King and gave not the least reason for assuming that he was connected with the last-mentioned. The only thing that happened that could give reason to thinking that such a connection existed was that Martin King at Slob, while he still was violent and wild, cried out to Bordeaux "I sent a message to you yesterday evening but got no answer." Because of that, Bordeaux wondered and answered that he had not received any message.

After that the previous explanation was read aloud to Mr. Major Gyllich who accepted the explanation as correct. He added that it seemed to him that Martin King, as he had joined him at Slob, said that there were large crowds on the road to Bass End, but he also assured that he had arranged that they turned back. The Major also added that it seemed to him as if Martin King on the mentioned day had had something to drink.

He remarks also, when asked, that he does not think that the negro Johannes from Bog of Allen was at Slob, as he knows him and did not see him there. In any case, the person questioned is certain that this negro, while the person questioned was there, did not take any active part in that which happened. While the person questioned was at Slob, no destruction happened.

Lieutenant Richard Beech

After that *Mr. Lieutenant R. Beech* from the Fire Brigade appeared. The explanation above given by Mr. Major Gyllich was read aloud to him. He confirmed that it was correct in every way, declaring that he all the time concerning continuously, was together with the Major.

As Mr. Beech had to leave the court for business for some moments, he left.

~~~~#~~~~

SUGAR MILL AT PLANTATION RUST-OP-TWIST

MEMBERS OF MARTIN KING'S "FLEET"

1. JOHANNES

2. WILHELM

3. ALEXANDER

4. RICHARD

5. ROBERT

6. JOSEPH

7. RANDAL

8. GEORGE WILLIAM

9. "LITTLE JIMMY"

ALL THESE MEN WERE OF THE SAME PLANTATION AS ADMIRAL MARTIN KING, PLANTATION BOG OF ALLEN.

CHAPTER IX

BUDDHOE'S CHRISTIANSTED IMPRISONMENT

THIS CHAPTER CONTAINS THE CHRISTIANSTED BOOKKEEPER H.M. Keutsch's Quarterly Expense Report with a column stating *"**Maintenance of the Negro Gottlieb (Buddo) in Christiansted fort, 139 days.**"*

It also contains an excerpt from Royal Councillor Bernhard von Petersen's writing, where he referenced General Buddhoe's time of imprisonment *(ibid, Page 136)*. There's also a translation dated July 24, 1848 when they moved General Buddhoe from Frederiks Fort to Christiansvaern Fort. He also received a passport to Tortola, which was later rescinded.

There's also a letter Irminger wrote to the Interim Governor-General with a list of items in General Buddhoe's possession as he boarded the *Ørnen*. These items included *"10 pieces of Eights"* which at the time was coin currency he could use in the British colonies. Buddhoe also had many letters of recommendation from both Danish officials as well as Planters. Irminger's intent was to notify the authorities of any and all of General Buddhoe's friends who were named in those letters.

Irminger took away all of Buddhoe's letters of recommendation to the Tortola authorities, hence demonstrating that he clearly had no intention of taking General Buddhoe to Tortola once the *"Ørnen"* left Christiansted harbor that December morning.

Maintenance of prisoners

Remuneration to government secretary for reduction of passports

King's treasury, taxes on courthouse

Hospital expenses for police servants

Repairs to courthouse

Light whilst cleaning public privies

Medicine for prisoners

Maintenance of the negro Gottlieb (Buddo) in Christiansteds fort, 139 days

Other expenses occasioned by the revolt

Inventory

Sundries

Station at Cliftonhill

1 police assistant, salary from 22d July 503 36

House rent 28 12

Maintenance of prisoners 71 42

Driver wages 18 72

Police servant, 10 days attendance during sickness of police assistant 18 72

A clock and a ream of paper 12 81

B. Frederiksted

AN ENTRY BY BOOKKEEPER KEUTSCH READS: "*MAINTENANCE OF THE NEGRO GOTTLIEB (BUDDO) IN CHRISTIANSVAERN FORT, 139 DAYS.*"

DANISH TEXT: Gottlieb Bourdeau. Opsendt I Aftes efter hr. Hoivelbaarenhed G. Gouverneurends Odrea med Lieutenant v. Holstein.

ENGLISH TRANSLATION: Gottlieb Bourdeau sent up this evening after His Excellence the Governor General's Order with Lieutenant v. Holstein.

Aarhus University
School of Culture and Society
Department of Archaeology and Heritage Studies
Postdoc – Enduring Materialities of Colonialism
"As scholars tasked with the important work of recounting the lived experiences of the oppressed and marginalized, we ought to "Pray for the Living and Fight LIKE HELL FOR THE DEAD." – Peter H. Wood

Captain Carl L.C. Irminger

No. 53

The war brig "Ørnen" [the Eagle] for anchor in St. Thomas the 14th December 1848.

Mr. General Governor!

Before leaving St. Thomas, I have the honor of informing you, Mr. General, about Buddo's having received a green suitcase with clothes and 10 pieces of Eights from St. Croix, I believe from Major Gyllich.

In the suitcase was a letter from some James W. Smith, which I thought proper to send to you, Mr. General. The writer of the letter, who might be able to give some information, is according to what Buddo said, a friend of his, who is employed by the Fire Corps at the West End.

Today I will finish the stocking up etc. and I sail either tonight or tomorrow.

Most humbly,

C. Irminger

To:
The General Governor of the
Danish West Indian Islands.

EXCERPT

As a lesser-known fact, I think it will perhaps interest the readers to learn how the Negro General Bordeaux fared. Buddoe (Gotlief) was a young man who had belonged to the owner of the Plantation La Grange. He did the whites a great service by betraying his comrades. He named the wildest and most dangerous rebels. But a natural consequence of this was that he was no longer sure of his life, and for that reason he placed himself under the protection of the Fire Brigade.

Major Gyllich was its Chief and when Buddoe had saved his life, the Major showed his gratitude by taking Buddoe home to his own house. The Fire Brigade must have sworn revenge on whoever dared lay hands on Buddoe.

In Christiansted, however, they wanted Buddoe removed from Frederiksted, as this man's presence in the future would become dangerous. Lieutenant v. Holstein was ordered to procure Buddoe for Christiansted by trickery or force, it didn't matter as long as you got him. This one, who knew that the Fire Corps took care that nothing approached Buddoe, Holstein, accompanied only by a Constable, but both well-armed, drove in an ordinary Phaeton to Frederiksted, got fresh horses at Frederiks Fort and now drove to the Major's residence.

To the Major he indicated that the Governor-General Chamberlain Oxholm wished to speak personally with Mr. Buddoe. The Major asked if Buddoe was under arrest since he had pledged his life with his own. To this, the Lieutenant replied that he was unfamiliar with the Governor-General's intentions. When the Major heard this, he demanded to drive along, which was granted. The Major sat with the Constable while Buddoe got a seat by the Lieutenant's side. The Constable had probably been instructed in case of any hostile demonstration and now it was galloping through the town. Lieutenant v. Holstein showed Buddoe then a cocked pistol with the remark "that he would be shot down at the first sign of any evasion," but everything went more calmly than was expected. No one noticed the abduction and the company soon arrived safely at Christiansted.

Buddoe entered the fort's prison accompanied by his protector, Major Gyllich, who would not leave his protégé, but shared his prison for several days. As it had to be admitted that the negro General had done more good than harm to the island, he was not subjected to any punishment, but was transported to one of the other West Indian islands.

The *Brig Ørnen* [Eagle], Captain Irminger, in the month of December was ordered to make a tour of the Windward Islands and South America, and the Captain was also given the task of taking Buddoe with him, as well as a colored man, Skelton, who had thrown poison into a well, from which the Spaniards took their drink. Governor-General Peter Hansen left the captain to put these two guys ashore where he had find best, but preferably in a place from which there was no great communication with the Danish Islands. Also, the Captain had the duty to interrogate Buddoe from time to time in order to possibly get him to confess who had actually given the idea for the riots on St. Croix.

They were handed over from the Fort in Christiansted on 13 December. Buddoe, a tall, strong-built negro, went on board, dressed like a gentleman, for many on island supported this rebel with money as well as clothes. On arrival on board, he brought with him several trunks containing new articles of clothing, some money and a number of letters from his friends. Captain Irminger said Buddoe was of the opinion that he should be taken to Tortola and there receive his freedom. Most of the letters therefore were letters of recommendation for him to people on that island and in several there were expressions such as "our friend, the governor general," or "General Buddoe" (our friend General Governor or General Buddoe).

Since there were also quite a few other persons' names in the letters and since it must have been based on authority in the future inquiries to get to know Buddoe's friends more closely, all the letters were sent to the Governor-General. Buddoe was naturally much offended by the captain's conduct in this respect.

From now on, Buddoe and Skelton were cared for on board as well as the crew. During the voyage, Buddoe several times asked Captain Irminger where he was to be taken and was told that it would partly depend on the information he gave regarding the negro riots. If he was open-hearted and confessed everything, they wanted to pardon him, otherwise things would go wrong for him.

Captain Irminger often interrogated him in his cabin, but he was so withdrawn that he never gave a single important piece of information. It was Captain Irminger's intention either to let him remain on Trinidad or to put him ashore on Paria, the country directly opposite this one, the land of burial for him.

On the 8th of January 1849, he landed in Port of Spain on Trinidad and Captain Irminger informed him that if he ever came back to the Danish-West Indian islands, he would have his life destroyed.

At Water-Gut Well Christiansted, St. Croix, D. W. I.

A PUBLIC WELL AT WATERGUT, CHRISTIANSTED

CHAPTER X

MARTIN KING'S CHRISTIANSTED IMPRISONMENT

THIS CHAPTER CONTAINS CHRISTIANSTED BOOKKEEPER H.M. KEUTSCH'S expense report with a column stating *"Reward for apprehending Martin King - 31.24."* There was a bounty on Martin King's head. He became a wanted man.

There's also a translation reflecting Martin King being transferred from Frederiks Fort to Christiansvaern Fort on the Schooner *"Vigilant"* on July 25, 1848. By this time, Admiral Martin King had turned himself in having been arrested on July 22, 1848.

There's also a translation where the Overseer Cooper of Plantation Negro Bay reported Martin King to the authorities in reference to a stolen boat from the bay.

Royal Councillor von Petersen wrote: *"Fortunately for Martin King, he was only arrested after the end of the Standard Courts. He was imprisoned for a couple of years and now occupies the modest position of a rat catcher on one of the northside plantations."*

the whole Rd 25 49 .... 274 11

MISCELLANEOUS

Travelling expences to public sales 18 81
Commission for collecting 281 56
Postage for ditto 16 70
Duty on Postage on same 10 58
Repairs of the wall around the churchyard
   at Christiansted 177 18
Constructing public well at Frederiksted 168 90
Surveying at Frederiksted 30

✓ Reward for apprehending Martin King 31 24

Provisions for refugees on board the vessels
   at Frederiksted during the disturbances 363 64
Drawing up a petition to the king respecting
   remuneration for losses sustained by the
   emancipation 312 18
Sundries 115 11   1,560 81

LOANS & OTHER TEMPORARY DISBURSEMENTS
To Poor Fund 2 000
Advances on salary 658 82
Purchase of corn meal 20,268 16
   ditto of hose for engines 110 10
Loans from Rum fund 500   21,037 12

Cash on hands 31st December 1848 .... 13 869 13

                                       105 070 12

Bookkeeper's Office, St. Croix 16th April 1849   H. M. KEUTSCH.

AN ENTRY BY BOOKKEEPER KEUTSCH READS: *"REWARD
FOR APPREHENDING MARTIN KING....31.24."*

PAGE 403 - (Dated July 17, 1848)

DANISH TEXT: Martin King, I Anledning af ham fremsod forvalterren af Plantagen Negrobay, Cooper og anmeldte at en der paa Bayen liggende Baad var bleven bortstjaalen, after Sigende af bemeldte Martin King, og at nogel dennes Klaedningsstykker vare fundne der paa Stedet, men at han Forvalterent, antog, at dette jun var skeet for at Vedkommde skulde antage at han var lobet bort fra Landet….

ENGLISH TRANSLATION: Martin King, in connection with whom the overseer of the Negro Bay Plantation, Cooper, appeared and reported that a boat lying on the bay had been stolen, allegedly by the said Martin King, and that some of his clothing had been found there on the spot, but that the overseer supposed that this had only been done in order that he might suppose that he had run away from the country….

Aarhus University
School of Culture and Society
Department of Archaeology and Heritage Studies
Postdoc – Enduring Materialities of Colonialism
"As scholars tasked with the important work of recounting the lived experiences of the oppressed and marginalized, we ought to "Pray for the Living and Fight LIKE HELL FOR THE DEAD." – Peter H. Wood

DANISH TEXT: Martin King, af Bog of Allen, afsendt med Skonnerten Vigilant til Commissionsretten I Christiansted.

ENGLISH TRANSLATION: Martin King, of Bog of Allen, sent with the Schooner *"Vigilant"* to the Commission Court in Christiansted.

Aarhus University
School of Culture and Society
Department of Archaeology and Heritage Studies
Postdoc – Enduring Materialities of Colonialism
"As scholars tasked with the important work of recounting the lived experiences of the oppressed and marginalized, we ought to "Pray for the Living and Fight LIKE HELL FOR THE DEAD." – Peter H. Wood

DANISH TEXT: Martin King fra Bog of Allen, opsendt hertil fra Commission in Frederiksted med Skrivelse ham vedkommende til Commissionen hersteds.

ENGLISH TRANSLATION: Martin King from Bog of Allen, sent here from the Commission in Frederiksted with a letter from him to the Commission here.

Aarhus University
School of Culture and Society
Department of Archaeology and Heritage Studies
Postdoc – Enduring Materialities of Colonialism
"As scholars tasked with the important work of recounting the lived experiences of the oppressed and marginalized, we ought to "Pray for the Living and Fight LIKE HELL FOR THE DEAD." – Peter H. Wood

CHAPTER XI

BUDDHOE'S 1840 AND 1841 ARRESTS

THIS CHAPTER CONTAINS A TRANSLATION OF GENERAL BUDDHOE'S arrests in both 1840 and 1841. According to the translation, Buddhoe was arrested and charged with "theft" on June 29, 1840 and rearrested November 19, 1840 for the same offence, for which he received 30 lashes. Then, on January 22, 1841 he was once again arrested and charged with "theft and maronloben" (meaning attempting to become a maroon). A translation of both the 1840 and 1841 arrest records are attached.

The 1840 Census classified him as "indifferent" with a notation of his arrests. According to one account, Buddhoe's father, John Gottlieb, had been tied to the wheel at Plantation La Grange for continuously attempting to escape. As a result, he was not given food on a regular basis as the others. General Buddhoe had stolen food (flour) to feed his elderly father.

General Buddhoe had done nothing for which he deserved to be so severely punished. To steal food out of the Master's kitchen to feed an elderly man who was unable to get food for himself is actually a selfless, compassionate and honorable thing to do. Truth be told, all of us would have done the exact same thing, if we had to, rather than watch our father starve to death. Therefore, he showed absolutely no dishonor by his actions. As for the "insolence" charge listed as a notation on the Census, I have thus far not been able to locate such.

THE 1840 CENSUS LISTING GENERAL BUDDHOE'S CHARACTER AS "INDIFFERENT" AND REFLECTING HIS IMPRISONMENT: "3 MONTHS IN THE NEW PRISON IN 1840 FOR THEFT AND 3 MONTHS 1841 FOR INSOLENCE. THE ABOVE PUNISHMENT INFLICTED BY JUDGMENT."

June 29, 1840

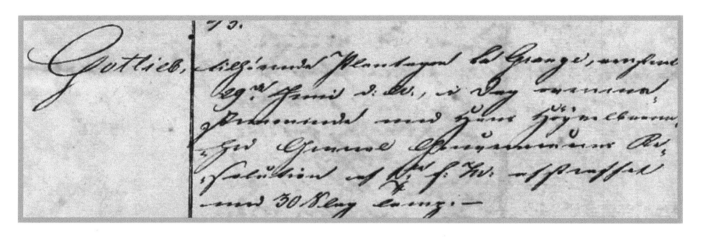

Translation: Gotlieb, belonging to the Plantation La Grange, arrested 29th June this year, to-day, according to the resolution of 1st last month by His Honor the General Governor, punished with 30 lashes.

~~~~#~~~~

November 19, 1840

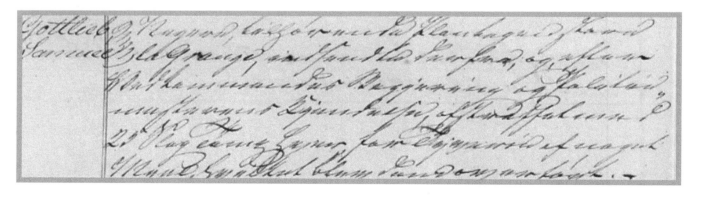

Translation: Gottlieb and Samuel, two negroes, belonging to the Plantation Great La Grange, picked up from there, and at request from the person concerned and at the written order of the Police Master, punished with 25 lashes each for theft of some flour, for which they were sentenced.

Danish Chancellery 5 – Criminal Reports West Indies

January 22, 1841

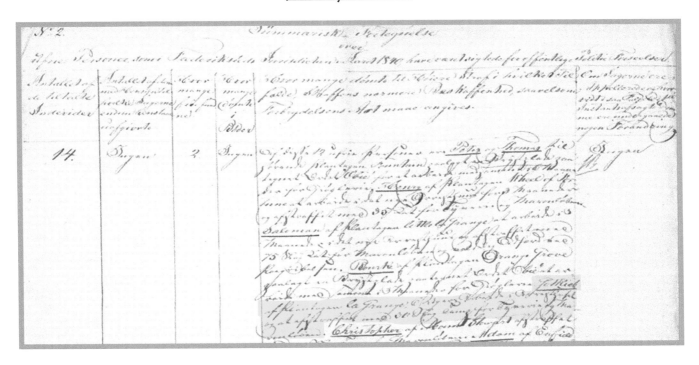

Translation: Gottlieb of the Plantation La Grange, six weeks work in the Arrest House and to be punished with 30 lashes for theft and "maronløben."[8]

---

8   According to the Danish dictionary Ordbog Over det Danske Sprog, the word "Maron" means 'a negro who has run away.' "Loben" means 'running.'

CHAPTER XII

CHRISTIANSTED'S TWO-DAY MASSACRE

THIS CHAPTER CONTAINS THE REPORT PREPARED BY LIEUTENANT ADAM McCutchin who was responsible for opening fire on the inhabitants in Christiansted on the night of July 3, 1848. It also contains a translation of the testimony of Lieutenant Louis Holstein who was responsible for opening fire on the inhabitants the day after on July 4, 1848, thereby causing Christiansted's two-day massacre. Major Falbe's testimony is also included.

Also, there's an excerpt of Governor-General Peter von Scholten's reaction to the massacre: *"The Governor-General realized that the dead had not even got to know that they no longer were slaves....!"* (ibid - *Page 405*)

An excerpt from the writings of Royal Councillor von Petersen describing the events of the Christiansted two-day massacre is also included. There's also from the records what seem to be a set of numbers, which seem to reflect a count of those killed in the Christiansted massacre.

A photograph of both Major v Falbe (who took over the affairs of Christiansted after Governor-General von Scholten's inability to do so) and Major v Gjellerup (who brought in prisoners to Christiansted on orders of the military command).

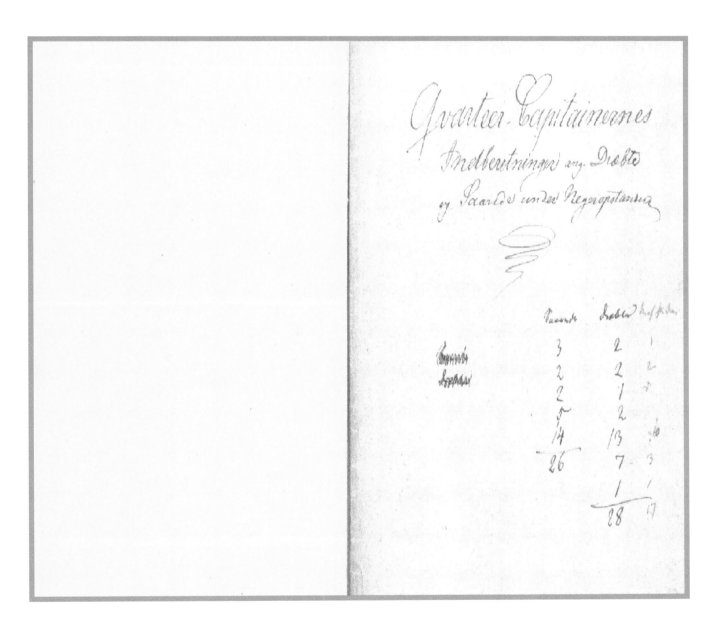

A VERY VAGUE LISTING OF POSSIBLE NUMBERS OF THOSE WOUNDED AND KILLED DURING CHRISTIANSTED'S TWO-DAY MASSACRE.

must be fired. The same minute that Falbe received this order a cannon shot followed by a series of volleys of musketry were heard from the western access route. The fort commander was not in doubt. Mac Cutschin was firing. That had to mean that the rebels were attempting to push into the town. Falbe decided to disregard the counter-order and fire alarm.

Scholten also heard the shots, first the cannon and then the discharge of lighter weapons from up the mountain road, shortly followed by the four roaring cannon-shots from the fort. He immediately got up, left his office, got hold of a horse and rode out to Mac Cutschin. The planter explained that a flock of nearly 200 Negroes had come against him with sugar-knives and truncheons, and that he had given the soldiers the order to open fire, with the result that the Negroes had fled. Scholten saw that the cannon had been loaded with grape shot and that the shot fired at close range had had a terrible effect. The road before him was covered with Negroes, some lay writhing with their bodies torn open by terrible wounds; others had been killed on the spot. The Governor-General realised that the dead had not even got to know that they no longer were slaves, lost his temper, turned to Mac Cutschin and laid into him. The tears stood in his eyes. Till now not a shot had been fired; he had given the slaves their freedom and it had not cost one drop of blood, this was a disgrace without equal, and the Negroes would take revenge. Had Mac Cutschin not heard about Martinique? Was he not aware that this could be the beginning of a massacre?

Scholten suddenly stopped, turned his back on the other, walked to his horse and rode slowly back to Christiansted, broken by over-exertion and inner misery. But his long working day was not over. He had to proofread and print the proclamation that made known that slavery had been abolished. In the late evening hours he sat once more at the oval mahogany table in the room where he had spent the previous night, together with a couple of civil servants had formulated the new regulations. The document was finished about midnight and was brought just across the street to the primitive printing press of the *St. Croix News*, where a couple of sleepy typographers were told to have as many copies as possible ready by sunrise.

105

AN EXCERPT HIGHLIGHTING GOVERNOR-GENERAL von SCHOLTEN'S REACTION TO THE CHRISTIANSTED MASSACRE.

EXCERPT

On General von Scholten's departure, he handed over the commando in Christiansted to Major v. Falbe, who immediately occupied the town's second entrance with artillery, West Indian infantry and militia; the northern entrance under Lieutenant McCutchin and the eastern under Lieutenant Rahr, both of the Militia. They received orders not to allow negro troops to enter the city and, if such, after being warned did not obey, then the grapeshot was to be used. Furthermore, the large prison was occupied by one non-commissioned officer and two men from Christiansted's Jaeger Corps.

At approximately six o'clock, General von Scholten returned from Frederiksted, after he had proclaimed the Emancipation of the negroes there. Major v Falbe now reported to the General what precautions he had taken, which were approved and he was allowed to fire the alarm to assemble the entire militia for the city's defense at night. At approximately seven o'clock, the General wanted the Major to carry out this order, but at the same moment he received orders to postpone this. When, however, at the same time he heard that cannon shots fell at the city's northern entrance, he immediately fired the three alarm shots in order to be able to gather the militia for the city's defense, as the same now seemed threatened.

Lieutenant McCutchin now reported that a negro troop of about 2,000 negroes had appeared and when, although warned several times, they continued to press on, they were received with shots by which some were killed and several wounded.

The negroes did not seem satisfied with this reception since they fled wildly across the country. It was later revealed that it had been their intention to set fire to the town and loot it. Although the negroes had achieved their wish to be free, they still continued on Tuesday the 4th to plunder and destroy everything on the plantations. General von Scholten, who did not want to allow Major v Falbe to advance against them, rode himself with his adjutant into the country, where he met several robbers who, after being exhorted by him, promised to go home, but no sooner had the General turned his back on them, before they had even begun the destruction.

It seemed to the citizens and Planters who fled to the city that this disorder should be remedied and they therefore turned to Major v Falbe that he should try to induce the General to take effective precautions. This one, who all day before had required the General to advance in the field against the negroes, which he was refused, now begged the citizens to be calm, promising them that he would renew his request again today, and immediately went to the General where, in the presence of Chamber Assessor Arnesen, he urgently demanded permission from the General to move out.

After complete resistance, it was granted to him on the condition that Assessor Rothe was to go along as a "civil commissioner" and that the Major had to promise not to shoot at the negroes. In the first case the Major agreed with ease; in the second only on the condition that if the negroes fired at him he would return fire. Assessor Arnesen immediately wrote down the instruction according to which the Major had to act. And as the latter believed that would have a good moral influence on the negroes when you appeared in the open field against them, he tried to admonish the General with every concession to that. Once he was out, his behavior had to depend mostly on the circumstances.

Major Falbe then received approximately two cannons, 60 cavalry from the Prince's Squadron and the Center Division, as well as approximately 140 men infantry, of which 24 was from the West Indian Infantry, the rest Militia from Christiansted's Brand Corps and Jaeger Corps.

With this commando, he marched off in the morning at nine and went out to the northside. The Planters overtook the Grande Princesse, St. John's, where a negro troop on horseback were engaged in plundering, and who, after having fired their guns at the cavalry, took flight in vain over the mountains, then marched over Montpellier, Morning Star and over the hills to Sion Hill and several plantations lying in the middle of the country.

The negroes, who in the morning had gathered about 3,000 men strong at Mon Bijou with the intention of again trying to surprise Christiansted, were soon informed of the troops' march, before they all went to their homes in the greatest haste and thus found the commando on every plantation it came to.

The negro population lined up, assuring the Major that they would behave calmly. In the evening at nine, the commando returned and the General appeared satisfied with what had been done.

However, the weather had not allowed it to show itself on the southside and the consequence of this was that they continued to loot there. The rumor of this continued disorder reached to town on Thursday morning, and when the General appeared early in the morning at the dockyard, he was received by several citizens and Planters who reproached him for his conduct, saying that if he did not immediately cut in more sharply, they must see that there's a second commander. The General tried to get rid of them and rode home as fast as possible, and when at the same time Major v Falbe wanted to go up to the Government House, these above-mentioned men came to him and said that they had told the General that they no longer wanted to recognize his commando, while they asked the Major to take over. This one sought to satisfy them, but was immediately ordered to the General, whom he found, partly after a difficult journey and partly after having for four days and nights of no rest, in a very weakened condition.

The General now handed over the commando to the Major, whom he asked to take Colonel Stadshauptmand de Nully as Assistant, whereas the Major could have no objection. It was now declared in a state of siege and a civilian council of several respectable officials was appointed to assist the military commando, especially in the supply of the troops.

The military commando now ordered Major v Gjellerup to move out with approximately a similar commando as the one that had been out the day before, with orders to, with the power to stop the unrest and to send in as prisoners the negroes who had shown themselves to be the most restless. The Major was also ordered to remain outside until all the disorder had stopped. At the same time, an order went to Frederiksted to send out similar patrol corps from there, which was most accurately carried out by Captain v Castonier.

In the course of Thursday and the whole of Friday, prisoners were now brought to Christiansted, so that both the fort and the prisons were overcrowded. And, finally, on Saturday morning, Major v Gjellerup arrived with his commando, carrying a number of prisoners, whose number now amounted to over 300.

The rebellion could now be considered ended and tranquility provided, so that Major v Falbe, after having suppressed this rebellion with his own forces, could receive the 600-man troops sent here from Puerto Rico with two mountain guns, as General Count Prim, then Spanish Governor-General on the island, with the same readiness and promptness had sent to St. Croix, with the happy news that calm had returned, but that their presence would be of great use in maintaining order.

Later in the day, in the evening, Colonel v Oxholm arrived at St. Croix, and on Sunday morning Colonel de Nully and Major v Falbe handed over the military commando to him, who, after General v Scholten, was now to act as Governor-General. Von Scholten travelled over to St. Thomas, returned to Denmark and, as it is well known, was brought before a Commission, which charged him with dereliction of duty, and they stripped him of his office as Governor-General of the Danish-West Indian islands. He appealed to the Supreme Court and was acquitted.

The rebellion was gradually put down, to which the presence of the Spanish troops significantly contributed. And on the 10th of July, the Planters were called to a meeting in order to draft new laws and determine the price of the work. Six Planters were selected to join the committee.

On a few plantations the work was now continued, but on most, the negroes would not order anything at all, when one did not want to give in to their unreasonable demands with regard to payment.

The result of the rebellion for those concerned in the country was that some plantations were completely looted; others had little furniture; sugar and rum stocks were partly destroyed and dressing gowns and the like were stolen. The tenements presented only a sad sight. The rudest vandalism had made its presence felt everywhere. In this way, for example, large mirrors were completely crushed. Finally, the fire had consumed a lot of sugar, store stocks and a lot of outhouses.

Before emancipation was declared, the slaves came forward with the consciousness that freedom was a right that belonged to them. While the behavior of the slaves thus had to testify to determination and confidence, the resistance had to become weaker, partly because many would be suspicious of and harbor a natural aversion to using violent means, where the object of the rebellion was only the acquisition of freedom. One is rightly surprised that the slaves were not led to more acts of violence with regard to the destruction of property or the sacrifice of life, which proves that a great religious influence has had an effect on their disposition.

Where has one seen an uprising of such a large number of people who belonged to the most ignorant working class, who had summoned power over the laws and the authorities who were in possession of many derelict properties, which in several places could rule over the lives of their masters and who finally possessed everything that could serve to excite their passions, without the most hideous results in acts of violence and murder having also appeared?

During the 29th of July, orders were issued to begin work on the plantations and no negro was allowed to leave the plantation he had previously belonged to. Several necessary precautions were also enforced. These only partially had a good outcome.

One longed for the new Governor-General from Denmark and the new regulations he reasonably brought with him, as the island's condition had now undergone such a significant change. Many despaired of Emancipation and predicted the island's ruin. Others were of good courage and believed that everything could still be turned for good.

First Lieutenant Adam McCutchin

Appeared *Merchant McCutchin*, Premier Lieutenant in the Infantry of the Militia in Christiansted (Christiansted's Division), and he explained that he Monday 3rd July in the afternoon appeared together with the company at which he is employed.

Major Falbe, who was then Commander-in-Chief, ordered the person questioned to fortify the western entrance to the city with a gun and some men, giving him the instruction that he, if the negroes should try to get in, should force them back, if necessary.

After that he took his post at the English church and set outposts. At eight – nine o'clock he heard from the highroad a noise, as from a large crowd, and therefore some managers from the country told him that the negroes had gathered in a large crowd outside the city. The outposts also reported that the negroes were coming. As far as the darkness allowed, the person questioned could see for himself large crowds. Because of this he ordered his men to be ready. He himself went ahead to meet the negroes, shouting to the negroes that they must stop, because otherwise they would be shot.

He assumes that the advancing crowd was about 60 or 70 paces from the entrance to the city, when he let the men shoot with rifles, though at first up into the air, but as the crowd kept advancing, he ordered a shot with the cannon and after that a volley with muskets.

After that was silence, and because of that he assumed that the negroes were retiring, which in fact was the case, for a patrol that he sent out found only wounded persons lying on the road. At the same time the alarm shots sounded from the fortress.

~~~~#~~~~

Premier Lieutenant Louis von Holstein

[This examination took place 2nd January 1849]

Appeared **Premier Lieutenant at the West Indian Infantry *von Holstein*,** explaining that he in the night between 2nd and 3rd July last year heard General Scholten outside the barracks calling on Major Giellerup, and because of that, the person questioned, who assumed that something unusual had taken place, got out of his bed, and dressed and went over to Major Giellerup, who in the meantime had talked to the General.

The person questioned was now ordered to keep the whole company at the Infantry ready for deployment and supply it with ammunition. But no appeal was allowed, the men had to be called together in silence, which was done immediately. But when it was five o'clock and no further orders had been given, the person questioned went to the Major asking if the men could take off their uniforms and drink tea. And when the Major had obtained the General's consent, they did so.

At seven o'clock it was entrusted to him by the Major to take the command of the detachment that was to move out. However, at the Government House he should get further order, and when he arrived there, General Scholten was standing at the stairs outside, ordering the person questioned with his detachment to take up a position at the Plantation Diamond & Ruby, occupying the road in the neighborhood and from there prevent the crowds of negroes penetrating in the direction of the city, but he must let a deputation of 8 – 10 people pass under escort.

He had with him 20 men regular infantry, 20 men militia hunters, a cannon with crew, and 20 men militia riders. He was specially instructed not to shoot unless he was resisted, or force was used against him.

At the mentioned plantation the person questioned held the position until Lieutenant Meincke arrived, going back from the West End and bringing the order to the person questioned from Colonel de Nully to go on to Frederiksted. However, the person questioned told Meincke, that he, before going to Frederiksted, wanted order as to this from the General. But as the land where he was standing was quiet, and as he could just as well fulfill the order at Kingshill, he went there. However, a short time later, the General arrived here on his way from Christiansted, ordering the person questioned to take up position at the Plantation Högensborg, because of which the person questioned alerted him, that it could not be avoided that here he came into conflict with the masses coming drunk back from Frederiksted. Because of that the General allowed that the person questioned went to Frederiksted.

Now he divided his company into two parts, let one part advance in front of the artillery, the other behind, requested carts to the footmen from the various plantations and arrived in the way quickly to the West End. However, there, the negroes had become emancipated before his arrival. He saw Strandgade filled with negroes, some of them drunk, from different places, and as the masses sometimes crowded very much upon him, he had to make the cannons ready for firing several times, but every time he did so, the negroes all the time moved away, and finally he arrived at the fortress.

Not much later, Lieutenant Woods, who commanded the Cavalry Department, reported to him that the negroes now had turned up in the neighborhood of Christiansted, and the person questioned informed the General of this. The General now went back to Christiansted, but before leaving he ordered the person questioned to stay in the fortress with the infantry.

The cavalry, on the contrary, which at first had been posted in the city, was ordered – except for six men who should be left with the person questioned – to go back to Christiansted in the evening that day. The person questioned drew attention to the fact that his detachment could have been conveyed there immediately with a schooner lying in Frederiksted, and so, without being out at night, at once could be used. But the General did not want this, but stuck to the order that he had given to the person questioned to march with his detachment back through the country to Christiansted early next morning.

During the night the person questioned sent out patrols and kept guard on one of the bastions, but as nothing happened and the war brig Ørnen [the Eagle] had assisted, the person questioned at three – four o'clock the next morning left for Christiansted. Until he came to Kingshill, everything was quiet, but at this side of Kingshill the negroes slowly began to gather behind the command, and when he came to Beeston Hill, he was totally surrounded by about 1,000 negroes, most of them with weapons.

Now he sent two negroes, who were standing on his way, to the crowds urging them to make the road passable, but the two negroes came back with the answer that they would not do him any harm, he could just march, after which he gave them the answer that this was not enough for him, they had to make the road free.

In the meantime, the stones flew over the head of the person questioned and his men from the hills around them, and because of that he ordered five – six men to cleanse the hills and ordered making the cannon ready. But when the first shot was fired from it, there was no change in the position of the negroes, as the person questioned had ordered, but, on the contrary, the negroes came closer, dancing and cheering.

The person questioned let another shot be fired by the cannon, and after that the whole crowd, when one person fell, immediately split. After that the person questioned, without further hindrance, could continue his way and arrived in Christiansted in the morning at about eight o'clock.

Later, the person questioned had been told that after the above-mentioned cannon shot and some musket shots there should have been three dead and some wounded.

After having returned here, the person questioned reported what had happened to the General when the General returned from the country, and he now politely reproached him for the shooting, saying that now he himself had made the negroes quiet, while the person questioned on the contrary had excited them, and now the person questioned was to blame for what happened next.

~~~~#~~~~

Christiansvaern Fort Commander Major Falbe

[1849, 14th March, the examination continued in the Government House]

Major Falbe appeared, remarking as to the statement given by General Scholten in his report of 13 August, that – which also can be seen from the explanation given earlier by the person questioned – the person questioned, and not the General, made the dispositions concerning the defense of the city of Christiansted that are mentioned in the said report and in the explanation of the person questioned.

When the General went to Frederiksted, he gave the person questioned the supreme command and told him to do the necessary, but he received no further special instructions. Wednesday in the morning at eight o'clock, the person questioned was ready to march with the artillery, though it is possible that the departure did not take place until later, but he is still convinced that they did not wait until 12 o'clock.

As to what happened at the Plantation St. John, he has, by and large, to agree with Lieutenant Bithorn's explanation. However, regarding the woman who was injured, it happened in the way that Chamberlain Rothe explained. It was a mulatto who is well-known in this country who injured the mentioned woman. The woman was brought to the hospital, where she was cured. The person who injured her, on the contrary, was delivered in this courthouse by the person questioned.

As to the end of Bithorn's explanation, the person questioned has to remark that he did not consider it prudent to allow himself to stay as long a time as it could take to catch the negroes concerned, which might have taken a long time because of the hilly terrain and the sugar fields. He considered it more important to get as far around as possible and especially go to the places where it was told that looting took place.

As to the sheep slaughterhouse at the Plantation Rattan, the person questioned must remark that he, when the negroes otherwise behaved calmly, could not feel empowered to step in with force against them according to his order, because it was said that the sheep had been stolen. An examination of this had, of course, to take place later by the competent authority.

[Read aloud and approved. The person questioned was permitted to leave].

CHRISTIANSTED NATIONAL HISTORIC SITE ALL SIX BUILDINGS

MAJOR ANTON ULRICH TROELS VINZEL FALBE
(1796 - 1865)

MAJOR CARL LUDWIG GJELLERUP
(1796 - 1876)

CHAPTER XIII

BRAND CORPS MAJOR JACOB HEITMANN GYLLICH

THIS CHAPTER CONTAINS A CENSUS REPORT OF MAJOR GYLLICH'S FAMILY from Plantation Stony Ground. Major Gylllich was Commander of the Brand Corps (which primarily comprised of free-coloureds).

Major Gyllich became a great help to both General Buddhoe and Admiral Martin King on the days following the Emancipation. He even allowed General Buddhoe to stay at his home until the Interim Governor-General Frederik Oxholm (who was the Governor on St. Thomas) used trickery to get Lieutenant Holstein to bring Buddhoe to Christiansted "for questioning," and later detained him.

General Buddhoe had saved Major Gyllich's life from an attack by a slave woman in Frederiksted with an axe, that would have beheaded Gyllich, "if she had good aim." As a result, Gyllich showed great endearing gratitude to General Buddhoe for his actions. When General Buddhoe was arrested and transferred to Christiansted, Major Gyllich would spend a few days with him in his prison cell, wanting to ensure for himself that no harm came to General Buddhoe.

Major Gyllich was born on St. Croix on March 28, 1795. He died on August 16, 1868 at the age of 73, and was buried in Lutheran Church Cemetery in Frederiksted. A picture of his gravestone is also included.

REGISTER

of Inhabitants living in the Country in

For Estate _Stony Ground_ in 8 West End Quarter No. 7 &c. belonging to M. H. Gyllich

Names of all persons living on the Estate.	Males.	Females.	Total.	Where born.	Age, fir running year in cluded.	Religion and when baptised.	Married, Widows, Single.	Widows, &c.	Each Persons Title, Office, Trade, Living, and relative state in the family.	Persons infected with the leprosy.
1. J. H. Gyllich	1			Africa	56	Lutheran	married		Major, Brandmajor of Works	
2. A. Gyllich		1		do	50	do				
3. M. M. Gyllich		1		do	28	do				
4. A. S. Gyllich		1		do	17	do			the Society	
5. C. E. Gyllich		1		do	16	do	unmarried			
6. A. N. Gyllich		1		do	14	do				
7. G. A. M. Gyllich	1			do	10	do				
8. G. C. Gyllich	1			do	6	do				
Servants										
9. Peter	1			do	24	english	unmarried		Groom	
10. Joseph	1			do	22	Moravian	do		Servant boy	
11. Andrew Barclay	1			do	30	do	do		Cook	
12. Francis	1			do	30	do	do		Houseservant	
13. Christina		1		Africa	30	english	do		do	
14. Mary		1		Africa	18	moravian	do		do	
15. Johan Simeon	1			do	27	danish Minnows	do		Shoemaker	
16. Victoria Richards		1		do	22	english	do		Seamstress	
Labourers										
17. William	1			do	40	roman Catholic	do		Labourer	
18. Martin James	1			do	40	english	married		do	
19. Peter James	1			do	28	do	unmarried		do	
20. Richard	1			do	22	moravian	do		do	
21. James	1			do	19	roman Catholic	do		do	
22. Joseph	1			do	20	do	do		do	
23. Bristol	1			Africa	65	english moravian	do		Watchman	
24. Peter	1			do	60	do english	do		do	
25. Geislen	1			Africa	18	do	do		Gardener	
Invalides										
26. Aline		1		Africa	70	danish Minnows	do		Invalide	
27. Elizabeth		1		Africa	76	do	do		do	

Stony Ground May 1850
Gyllich

THE 1850 CENSUS OF MAJOR GYLLICH AND HIS FAMILY OF STONY GROUND, FREDERIKSTED.

MAJOR JACOB HEITMANN GYLLICH'S GRAVE STONE
HOLY TRINITY LUTHERAN CHURCH CEMETERY - 1868

CHAPTER XIV

THE GUNPOWDER

THIS CHAPTER CONTAINS INFORMATION ON THE GUNPOWDER AVAILABLE in Frederiks Fort on the day of the Emancipation according to the Fort Commander Castonier, who later gave a report to the Government Commission investigating the Emancipation events.

Commander Castonier reported that there was 2,319 pounds of gunpowder available, *more than enough for defense of the city.* (ibid, *Page 373, Hansen*)

There's also a Plan of Frederiks Fort from 1780 which includes the "vaulted" Powder Magazine in which the gunpowder would have been stored. Also included is a sketch of Christiansvaern Fort Powder Magazine room with storage barrels demonstrating how the gunpowder was stored.

Also, the following testimony was given by First Lieutenant Meincke as it relates to the amount of gunpowder at Frederiks Fort on July 3, 1848:

"When they were present in the fortress of Frederiksted January 1st last year, apart from 1,620 pounds cannon gunpowder and 699 pounds of musket powder, furthermore, 925 sharp rifle cartridges, 576 sharp pistol cartridges and 2,658 sharp musket cartridges, of which quantity now the main part must have been left, when the unrests broke out." [ibid, See Page 35 - Meincke].

Adding the 1,620 and the 699 pounds of gunpowder, this equals to the number given by *Hansen* of 2,319 pounds of gunpowder being available.

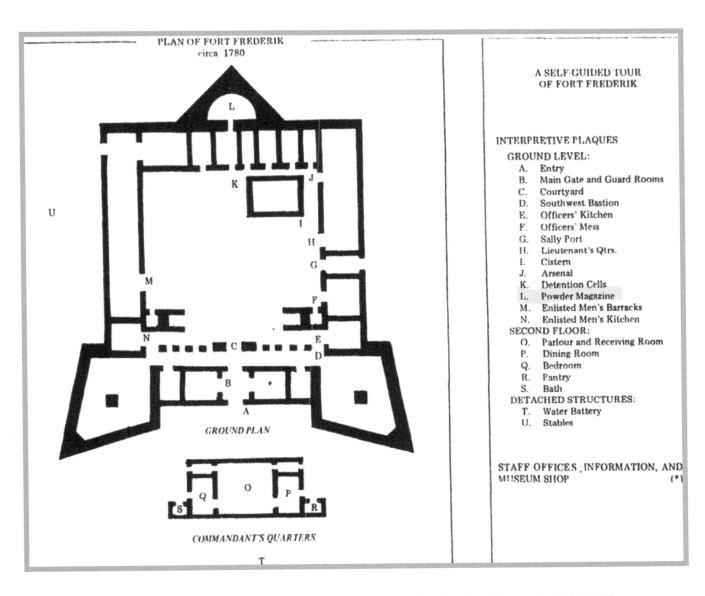

PLAN OF FREDERIKS FORT SHOWING POWDER MAGAZINE
(L) AT A TRIANGULAR-SHAPED PROJECTING SALIENT.
(*NATIONAL PARK SERVICE, ATLANTA*)

Describe Present and Historic Physical Appearance.

Fort Frederik is a mid-eighteenth century Danish masonry fort located at the north end of Frederiksted, on the western end of St. Croix, United States Virgin Islands. The fort was to protect Danish colonial interests in the Caribbean and the western end of St. Croix against incursions by other colonial powers, prevent smuggling, protect shipping in the Frederiksted harbor, and maintain order among the plantation slaves. The fort is slightly trapezoidal in plan, with diamond-shaped bastions at the southwest and northwest corners, and a triangularly-shaped projecting salient on the east side that housed the powder magazine. Within the curtain, or long walls, of the fort are a number of rooms which functioned as Officer's and Men's Kitchens and Rooms, and Detention Cells, all opening on to an inner brick-paved courtyard. The Commandant's Quarters, the only second story part of the fort, was built above the main entrance on the west, or seaward side, of the fort. Exterior stairs provide access to the Commandant's Quarters and the roof of the first level of the fort which also held gun batteries. On the west side, is a three pointed masonry sea battery, and on the north side are the masonry stables, enclosed by a masonry wall (see Figures 1-3; see Photos 1-4).

FREDERIKS FORT VIEW LOOKING WEST AT SEA BATTERY.

FREDERIKS FORT VIEW FROM ROOF TO THE WESTERN PART OF FORT LOOKING NORTH AT STABLES.

THE POWDER MAGAZINE ROOM AT CHRISTIANSVAERN FORT DEPICTING HOW THE GUNPOWDER WAS STORED BENEATH THE WATER BATTERY.

they got transferred, who looked after themselves and were not afraid of being bored. Sure enough, Captain Castonier, the officer in charge of the fort later declared with dramatic military huff, that his fort had been short-staffed and poorly armed. But that was not true. There was the number of soldiers that was supposed to be there, and there were also enough gunpowder and bullets. It was Captain Castonier who, if truth be told, was not a very courageous man. And the town's police chief, "Old Andresen", as he was called? Alas, old Andresen was no older than 66 years, but a long life in the tropics had taken its toll, and now Andresen was actually somewhat frail, well-meaning, but confused and helpless, senile as a ninety-year-old. The head of the fire brigade, on the other hand, showed more energy, the young Major Gyllich, who was in charge of an elite force of 270 free Coloured armed with 62 guns and 50 swords. But the major had the reputation of being a

neck. The big blow somehow missed. Gyllich shouted that he was their friend, not their enemy, threw as proof his sword down and said they could take his life if they wished. The major knew the Negroes, this daring gesture saved him, and Gyllich was allowed to pass. Before the house of Frederik von Scholten, the street was packed with slaves who demanded their freedom; the inspector of taxes had to come to the window and try to get them to keep order, but was soon interrupted with shouts of "Massa Peter". Frederik von Scholten tried to be heard: He had written to his brother! The Governor-General would come!

Most of the rebels, men, women and children gathered together at the large open square before the fort. Castonier, who was in charge, did not quite know what to do. He had 48 men at his command, who after the Negro revolt on the French islands had further been strengthened with 16 infantry soldiers. The little fort had no less than 32 cannons and according to the inventory, he had 2319 pounds of gunpowder, 3543 rifle cartridges and 150 pieces of cannon balls – more

THESE EXCERPTS REPORTED THERE WAS ENOUGH GUNPOWDER FOR DEFENSE OF THE CITY OF FREDERIKSTED ON JULY 3, 1848.

CHAPTER XV

LIST OF THOSE ARRESTED, ACQUITTED, SENTENCED AND SHOT

THIS CHAPTER CONTAINS A COMPLETE LIST OF THOSE WHO WERE ARRESTED, acquitted, questioned, sentenced and shot on both July 3rd and 4th 1848. There are some who were wounded on July 3rd or 4th, but did not die until days or weeks later on their respective plantations. An excerpt from the *"Record of Deaths"* of Christiansted's English Church is also attached.

This list contains all those arrested and questioned from the various plantations. The interrogations went on for approximately five weeks. The names of those executed in Christiansted's two-day massacre have not yet been found, except for the few names on the *Record of Deaths* (Josephine, William, Andreas, Stephanus, George and Joe). The list reflects a total of 17 who were immediately executed in Frederiksted, during the court-martial examinations:

224 were arrested, questioned and acquitted, which included 47 women; and

There was (1) gentleman, Samuel Ephraim, who was listed in the records as having *"cut his own throat while in prison."*

By the time of the Commission investigations in 1849, there were a plantation-by-plantation report that was requested for the Planters to submit the names and ages of anyone killed and/or wounded on their respective plantations.

Those arrested, questioned, sentenced, and shot:

NAME	PLANTATION
Simon	Cane Bay
Pompey	Prosperity
Martin	Jolly Hill
George Williams	Butler's Bay
Martin King**	Bog of Allen
Johannes	Negro Bay
Martin Williams	Hams Bay
Joe aka Joseph	Hard Labor
Ludvig aka Daco	Cane Bay
James Heyliger	Enfield Green
Moses Robert	Butler's Bay
George Fancy	Butler's Bay
C. Lucas	Mt. Pleasant
Decatur	Lower Bethlehem
Adam	Rosehill
Augustus	Concordia
Henry	La Reine
Friday	Castle

**[Martin King initially escaped the evening of the examinations]*

Those questioned and acquitted:

	NAME	PLANTATION
1.	Johnny	Mannings Bay
2.	Gotlieb	Mannings Bay
3.	Sarah*	Mannings Bay
4.	Robert	Mannings Bay
5.	Johannes	Mannings Bay
6.	George	Mannings Bay
7.	Presley	Mannings Bay
8.	Sally*	Mannings Bay
9.	Lydia*	Mannings Bay
10.	Eva*	Mannings Bay
11.	Adelaide	Mannings Bay
12.	John Cornelius	Mannings Bay
13.	James	Mannings Bay
14.	Jonas	Butler's Bay
15.	Michel	Butler's Bay
16.	Charles	Butler's Bay
17.	Josiah	Spratt Hall
18.	Ottar	Spratt Hall
19.	Johannes	Spratt Hall
20.	George Taylor	Spratt Hall
21.	Benn	Spratt Hall
22.	Vincent	Spratt Hall
23.	Franky	Spratt Hall
24.	John James	Spratt Hall
25.	Bella*	Spratt Hall
26.	Else*	Spratt Hall
27.	Andreas aka Cuby	Envy
28.	Hans	Envy
29.	William Thomas	Envy
30.	Lorentz	Envy
31.	Moses	Envy
32.	George	Mountain
33.	Abraham	Mountain
34.	Billy	Mountain
35.	Jeremiah aka John Meyer	La Grange

36.	Henry Daniel	La Grange
37.	Rudolph	La Grange
38.	Bertha*	La Grange
39.	William	Little La Grange
40.	Andrew	Little La Grange
41.	Battist	Carlton
42.	Joseph	Carlton
43.	Cathrine*	Carlton
44.	Samuel	Carlton
45.	Alexander	Carlton
46.	October	Concordia
47.	Norah*	Concordia
48.	Bok	Concordia
49.	Benjamin	Concordia
50.	Andreas	Concordia
51.	Ludvig	Concordia
52.	Ruby*	Concordia
53.	Rachel*	Concordia
54.	Sacky	Concordia
55.	Kate*	Concordia
56.	Cancer	Mt Washington
57.	Henry	Mt Washington
58.	Hester	Mt Washington
59.	Allick	Mt Washington
60.	John	Campo Rico
61.	Samuel	Campo Rico
62.	Isaac Ferdinand	Prosperity
63.	Patrick	Prosperity
64.	Martin	Hams Bay
65.	Martin William aka Charles Martin	Hams Bay
66.	William Johnson	Hams Bay
67.	Adam Charles	Wheel of Fortune
68.	Martin	Wheel of Fortune
69.	Lena*	Wheel of Fortune
70.	Margreth*	Wheel of Fortune
71.	Rebekka*	Wheel of Fortune
72.	Ann*	Wheel of Fortune
73.	Sally*	Wheel of Fortune

74.	Beth*	Wheel of Fortune
75.	Maria*	Wheel of Fortune
76.	Louisa*	Mt Pleasant
77.	William Jones	Mt Pleasant
78.	Andreas	Mt Pleasant
79.	Beatrice*	Mt Pleasant
80.	Frederik aka Bongo	Mt Pleasant
81.	Matthew	Grove Place
82.	William	Grove Place
83.	Felicia*	Grove Place
84.	Malvina*	Grove Place
85.	Phillipus	Grove Place
86.	Neddy*	Grove Place
87.	Robin*	Negro Bay
88.	Jonathan	Negro Bay
89.	Joseph	Negro Bay
90.	Lucky*	Negro Bay
91.	Louisa*	Negro Bay
92.	Rosina*	Negro Bay
93.	Salomon	Negro Bay
94.	Aletta*	Negro Bay
95.	James	Negro Bay
96.	Johan	Negro Bay
97.	Quamina*	Bethlehem
98.	Bernie	Bethlehem
99.	John Richard	Mt Stewart
100.	John David	Mt Stewart
101.	Christopher	Mt Stewart
102.	Benjie	Mt Stewart
103.	William	Mt Stewart
104.	George	Mt Stewart
105.	David	Mt Stewart
106.	Peats	Upper Love
107.	Billy	Upper Love
108.	Joseph	Upper Love
109.	Thomas	Upper Love
110.	John	Upper Love
111.	Charles	Upper Love

112. Plato .... Upper Love
113. Joseph .... Bog of Allen
114. Phillip .... Bog of Allen
115. Jacob .... Bog of Allen
116. Robert .... Bog of Allen
117. Wilhelm .... Bog of Allen
118. Johannes .... Bog of Allen
119. Richard .... Bog of Allen
120. Alexander .... Bog of Allen
121. Robert .... Paradise
122. Sam .... Paradise
123. Andrew .... Paradise
124. Jacob .... Plessen
125. Emanuel .... Plessen
126. Edward .... Bettys Hope
127. Paddy .... Bettys Hope
128. Robert Lucas .... Bettys Hope
129. George .... Enfield Green
130. Peter .... Enfield Green
131. William .... Enfield Green
132. Moses .... Enfield Green
133. Andrew .... Enfield Green
134. Andreas .... Nicholas
135. Sacky .... Nicholas
136. Andrew .... Nicholas
137. Gustus .... Spring Garden
138. Henry .... Spring Garden
139. Kitt* .... Spring Garden
140. Matthias .... Spring Garden
141. Seth .... Spring Garden
142. Joshua .... Spring Garden
143. Didrik .... Spring Garden
144. Billy .... Spring Garden
145. Francis .... Spring Garden
146. June* .... Spring Garden
147. Peter .... Spring Garden
148. Moses Hewlett .... Spring Garden
149. Jim .... Spring Garden

150. George .... Spring Garden

151. Charles .... Spring Garden

152. Lucretia* .... Spring Garden

153. Nicholas... Spring Garden

154. James Phaire .... Spring Garden

155. Anthony .... Lower Love

156. Thomas .... Lower Love

157. Josiva* .... Lower Love

158. Miriam* .... Good Hope

159. William Peebles .... Good Hope

160. Caesar .... Good Hope

161. Big Frederick .... Big Fountain

162. Lucas aka Lee .... Big Fountain

163. John Simmons .... Big Fountain

164. Frederik .... Big Fountain

165. Charles .... Big Fountain

166. Sam .... Big Fountain

167. Paddy .... Big Fountain

168. Josett* .... Big Fountain

169. Malvina* .... Big Fountain

170. Smart .... Big Fountain

171. Henry .... Montpellier

172. Jane* .... Montpellier

173. Albert .... Montpellier

174. Charles .... Montpellier

175. Cornelius.. Montpellier

176. Sam .... Montpellier

177. Frederik .... Montpellier

178. Henry .... Anguilla

179. Cornelius.. Anguilla

180. Joseph .... Anguilla

181. William .... St Georges

182. Catherine* .... St Georges

183. John Morton .... St Georges

184. Caesar .... St Georges

185. Cheddrik .... St Georges

186. Henry .... St Georges

187. Johannes... Hard Labor

188. Paulus .... Hard Labor
189. Joseph .... Rosehill
190. Richard .... Rosehill
191. John William .... North Star
192. Andrew .... North Star
193. William .... North Star
194. Johnson .... North Star
195. Michael .... Adventure
196. William .... Adventure
197. Present* .... Jealousy
198. Thomas Clarke .... Jealousy
199. Bastian .... La Vallee
200. Frederick .... Retreat
201. William aka Dick .... River
202. Penny* .... River
203. Peter .... Fredensborg
204. Sipio .... Cane
205. Francis .... Hogensborg
206. Frederik .... Waldegaard
207. Plato .... Windsor
208. Jimmy .... William's Delight
209. Johannes .... Mon Bijou
210. Margaret Johnson* .... Frederiksted
211. Madelaine* .... Punch
212. Sofie* .... Rust-Op-Twist
213. Irwin King .... Cane Garden
214. Charles .... Oxford
215. Lucretia* .... Diamond & Ruby
216. Charlie .... Sion Farm
217. Richard .... Two Friends
218. Friday .... Castle Burke
219. Berne .... Two Williams
220. Balfour .... La Reine
221. Eveline* .... Lundegaard
222. Christian .... D Worm (owner)
223. Rosalina* .... Jackson (owner)
224. John Francis .... Jackson (owner)

* = [Women]

.	16.	. .	Richmond	16 July 1848	child
.	16.	"	Alexander	16 July 1848	child
.	18	Piedmont	Benjamin	25 May 1799	Priscilla, Cas...
	19	Bohemia	Andreas	25 Jan 1822	unmarried
.	22	Annerhope	Magdalena	6 Feb. 1791	Wilhelm, Mon...
.	27	Castle Coakley	Johann Martin	20 Oct. 1805	Widower.

1840		child		1 day
1848		child		1 day
1799	Priscilla, Castle Coakley	Piedmont		21 years
1822	unmarried	Work and Rest		21 - from his wounds
1791.	Wilhelm, Mountainhill	Annerhope		57 - fever
1805.	Widower.	Castle Coakley		62 -

**ANDREAS (AGE 19) OF PLANTATION WORK & REST,
DIED *"FROM HIS WOUNDS"* JULY 4, 1848.**

STEPHANUS (AGE 34), WHO WAS A FIELD LABORER ON PLANTATION DIAMOND, *SHOT IN THE NEIGHBORHOOD OF BASSIN* (CHRISTIANSTED) JULY 4, 1848.

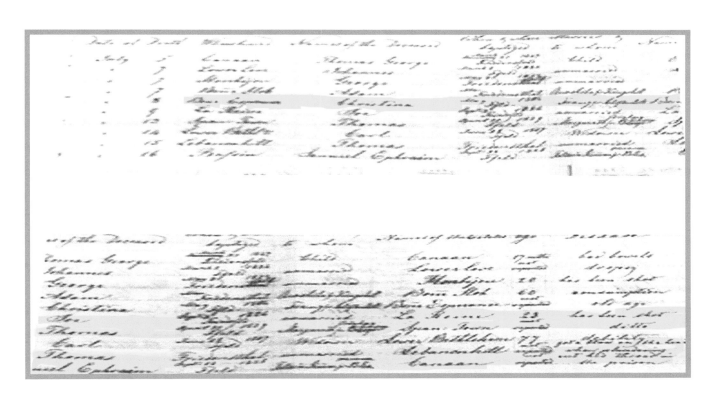

ON JULY 4, 1848:

GEORGE (AGE 20) OF PLANTATION MON BIJOU *"HAS BEEN SHOT."*

JOE (AGE 23) OF PLANTATION LA REINE *"HAS BEEN SHOT."*

**THOMAS (AGE NOT REPORTED) OF PLANTATION LEBANONHILL
*"GOT A BLOW TO THE HEAD WHEN PLUNDERING."***

**SAMUEL EPHRAIM (AGE NOT REPORTED) OF PLANTATION
CANAAN *"CUT HIS THROAT IN THE PRISON."***

Date of Death		Where Burried	Names of the Diseased	Where Baptized	Married or Unmarried		Age	Disease	Situation Rank Profession	Remarks
1848 July	4	Church Yard	Josephine	Eng Church	Unmarried		30	Wounded on the night of the 3rd	Labourer on Estate Castle Coakley	
"	10	Church Yard	Harry	"	" "		59	Debility		
"	12	" "	Mrs Downing	"	Married		30	Consumption		
"	13	" "	William	"			1 day			
"	13	" "	William	"	Unmarried		40	Wounded on the night of the 3rd	Labourer on Estate La Reine	
"	13	" "	Frances	"	"		1 day			
"	16	Estate Hamburg	Mary	"	" "		5 mths	Consumption		
"	18	Estate Castle Coakly	Caalina	"			6 ?	Bowels		

JOSEPHINE (AGE 30) OF PLANTATION CASTLE COAKLEY
"WOUNDED ON THE NIGHT OF THE 3RD."

WILLIAM (AGE 40) OF PLANTATION LA REINE
"WOUNDED ON THE NIGHT OF THE 3RD."

CHAPTER XVI

BUDDHOE'S ASSASSIN (CARL LUDVIG CHRISTIAN IRMINGER)

THIS CHAPTER CONTAINS INFORMATION AND A PHOTOGRAPH OF THE person I refer to as "Buddhoe's assassin," Carl Ludvig Christian Irminger. He sailed the *Brig-of-war Ørnen* with Buddhoe on board from St. Croix on December 13, 1848 but never listed a specific destination for the *brig.* Irminger would later be given a "golden saber" by a group of Planters on St. Croix upon his return to the island after sailing to "wherever" with General Buddhoe on board. Could this have been a reward for his dastardly deed of allegedly throwing General Buddhoe overboard somewhere in the middle of the ocean?

This Chapter also includes information on Irminger's exploits at "Fort Prinzenstein" in Keta, Ghana where he opened fire from the "*Ørnen*" on the inhabitants who were leading a local revolution in 1847-1848 and had locked a Danish official in the citadel. Irminger would also be the one to declare "martial law" during the time of von Scholten's inability to govern the DWI, thereby allowing many to be arrested and shot. Upon his declaration of martial law he issued a Proclamation which stated, in part that: *"they* [the negroes] *would be fired upon from His Majesty's Ørnen."*

Irminger was born on April 3, 1802 in Wewelsfleth and died on February 7, 1888 in Copenhagen at the age of 85. He was married to a woman by the name of Henriette.

CAPTAIN CARL LUDVIG CHRISTIAN IRMINGER

148

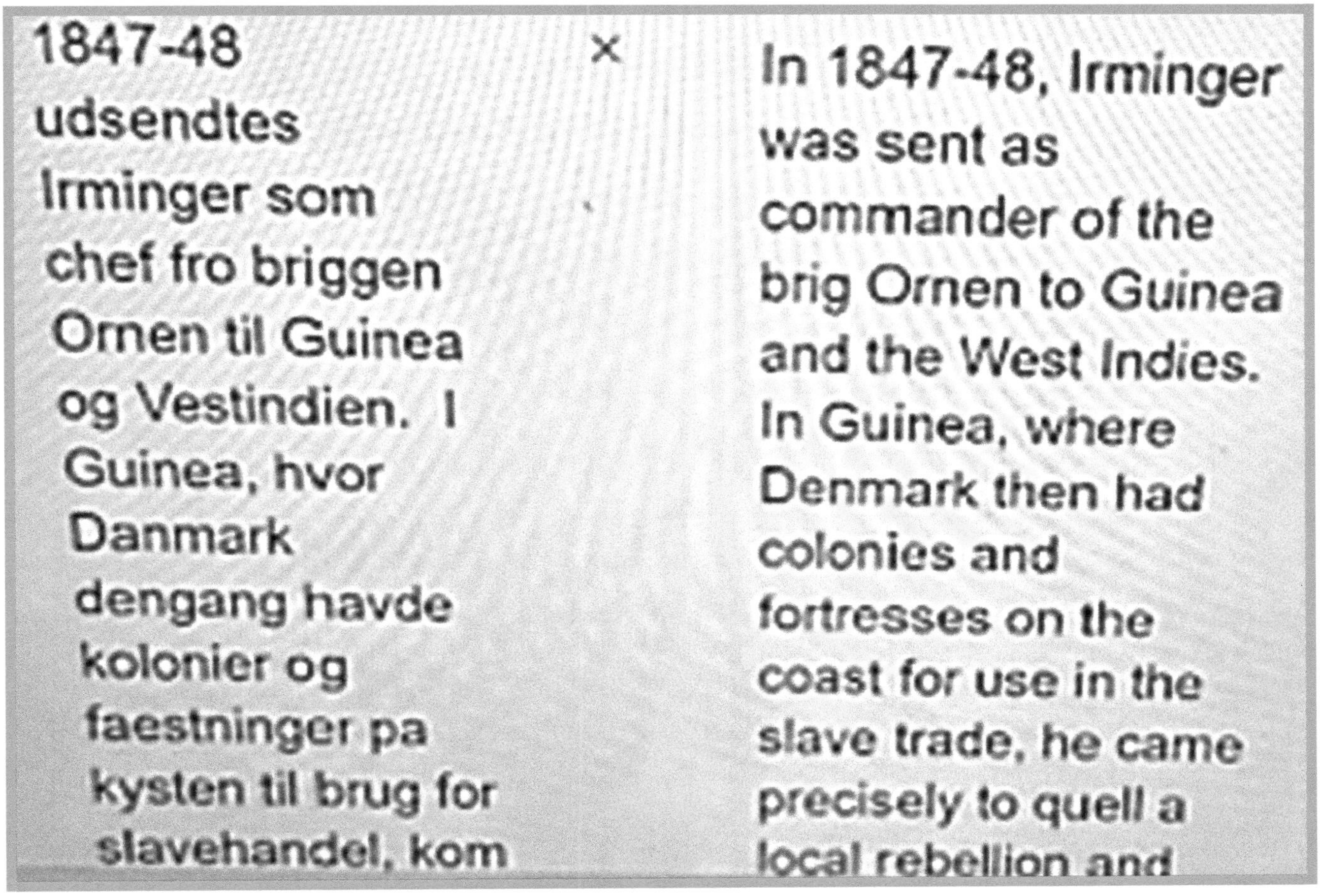

1847-48
udsendtes
Irminger som
chef fro briggen
Ornen til Guinea
og Vestindien. I
Guinea, hvor
Danmark
dengang havde
kolonier og
faestninger pa
kysten til brug for
slavehandel, kom

x

In 1847-48, Irminger
was sent as
commander of the
brig Ornen to Guinea
and the West Indies.
In Guinea, where
Denmark then had
colonies and
fortresses on the
coast for use in the
slave trade, he came
precisely to quell a
local rebellion and

THE FOLLOWING THREE PAGES IS A DANISH-TO-ENGLISH DESCRIPTION OF CAPTAIN IRMINGER'S EXPLOITS IN KETA, GHANA WHERE HE QUELLED A LOCAL REBELLION BY FIRING FROM THE BRIG-OF-WAR *ØRNEN* ON THE INHABITANTS, KILLING THOUSANDS.

faestninger pa kysten til brug for slavehandel, kom han netop telpas for at daempe et lokalt opror og frelse den dervaerende lojtnant Svedstrup som var blevet indusluttet pa citadellet pa Prinsensten. Under Ornens ophold i Vestindien (juli

slave trade, he came precisely to quell a local rebellion and save the then lieutenant Svedstrup who had been locked up in the citadel on Prinsensten. During Ornen's stay in the West Indies (July 1848) there was also an uprising among the slaves of the plantation owners, which ended with Peter von Scholten's dissolution of Danish-

Vestindien (juli 1848) upbrod ogsa der opstand blandt plantageejernes slaver, des endte med Peter von Scholtens oplosning af dansk-kontrolleres slaveri 3. juli 1848. Kaptainlojtnant Irminger erklarede Frederiksted i undtagelsestilsta

dissolution of Danish-controlled slavery on 3 July 1848. Captain Irminger declared Frederiksted in a state of emergency and began to arrest what he believed to be troublemakers and hold court trials. [Peter von Scholten himself had suffered a stroke and was close to death. Against Peter von Scholten's order, there were skirmishes all

Frederiksted i undtagelsestilsta nd og begyndte at fange, hvad han mente, var urostiftere og lave standretter. [Peter von Scholten selv havde faet et slagtilfaelde og var doden naer. Mod Peter von Scholtens ordre var der traefninger rundt omkring. hvor hvide skod pa de ubevaebnede sorte. Da der igen begyndte at komme ro pa oerne, blev tavene opgjort til i alt 40 draebte. Alle var sorte, og ikke en eneste

there were skirmishes all around, where whites shot at the unarmed blacks. When calm began to return to the islands, the toll was calculated at a total of 40 killed. All were black and not a single one was white. The plantation and slave owners subsequently recognized Irminger by presenting him with a valuable gold sable. When the brig returned in 1849, Irminger remained on board as commander and participated with it in the blockade in Ostersoen.

CHAPTER XVII

THE BRIG-OF-WAR "ØRNEN"

THIS CHAPTER CONTAINS A PHOTOGRAPH OF THE *BRIG-OF-WAR ØRNEN* AS it was in 1848 berth right off of Protestant Cay (Hotel on the Cay) in the Christiansted harbor. Irminger wanted to take drastic action in Frederiksted and execute over 8,000 of our ancestors who assembled on July 3, 1848 for their Emancipation. Thankfully, he was prevented by the Governor-General from taking the *Ørnen* to Frederiksted in advance of the Governor-General getting there. *[See Chapter XV]* The *Ørnen* carried 16 cannons.

Also, this Chapter contains the relevant outgoing shipping records of the *Brig-of-war Ørnen* in 1848. On one departure record, Irminger listed "*Islands*" and on the other "*Laredo Peru*" was listed. Why not list a specific destination? Where was he really taking General Buddhoe on the *Ørnen*? This question remains unanswered.

However, it is worth noting that Lt. Petersen in his report wrote that Buddhoe was put ashore at "*Paria*" (an uninhabited island off the coast of Port of Spain, Trinidad). It is said that Irminger gave up on interrogating General Buddhoe in the cabin of the *Ørnen* on January 8, 1949, having interrogated him every day for 25 days on board.

Irminger named a sea for himself in the North Atlantic bordering Greenland – Irminger Sea. He would later become the Danish Vice Admiral and Minister of the Danish Royal Navy.

HIS MAJESTY'S BRIG-OF-WAR ØRNEN SAILING ON THE OCEAN.

Briggen, Ørnen

**THE *ØRNEN* AS IT WAS ANCHORED IN CHRISTIANSTED HARBOR
ADJACENT TO PROTESTANT CAY (HOTEL ON THE CAY).**

Shipping (West Indies)

Government-General, St. Thomas Harbour Master: Pilot journals of outgoing vessels (1821 - 1865)

Contents

1821

1833 -1835

1840 -1843

1843 -1848

1848 -1853

1855 -1858

1858 -1862

1862 -1865

Eng. schr. Argo, Nickerson, do Sth.
Eng. brig Fergus, Brown. Grangemouth, coals.
Dan. schr. Vigilant, Nielsen, St. Croix. blt.
Dan. schr. Genl. v. Scholten. McGregor, do do.
Dan. schr. W.E. Packet, Higgins, do do.
15.—Eng. sloop Aurora, Beal, St. Barths.
Eng. brignt Nova Scotia, Brine, St. Martin.
American schr. Leprelett, Sleeper, St. Kitts.
American barque Tivoli, Wheeler, Guadeloupe,
   lumber.
English brig Penyame, Hale, Newport. coals.
American schr. Genl. Morgan, Falenberg, St.
   Martin, salt.

CLEARED.

13—French brignt Alexandre, Charles, Naguabo.
British sloop Lydia, Ritchie, Antigua.
Venez. schr. Gratioso, Romney, La Guayra.
14—French do Perseverance, Edmond, Guadeloupe,
   imported.
Eng. brignt Ranger, Paynter, Mayaguez, impt.
Bremen brignt Dettmar, Oasen, Pto Plata.
Span. barque Dominga, Sato, Fazardo, provision.
15—Dan. schr. St. Croix, Coker, St. Croix, drygoods
Dan. brig of war Ornen, Irminger, Islands.
Eng. steamer Thames, Abbot, Southampton.
French brig La Perle, Boyer, Marseille.
Eng. barque James Ewing, Maitland, PtoPrince.
   imported.
Eng. do Recovery, Burke, New Orleans.
Eng. brigt Economist, Perry, Norfolk.

THE TIMES.

geria for instance). ...
are the real difficulties
legislators of the your
have to grapple—seriou
trust for the sake of
tion and social progres
table. In Austria, tr
triumphant, and the R
na completely quelle
but how long tranquil
be maintained in that
posed of so many ant
such different stage
problematical; in the
ry despotism is not
necessary for the we
In Prussia we regret
not much better.
clared in a state of
immense military p
collision was appreh
populace and the tr
empire at present i
standing its Parli
Frankfort is making
towards consolidation
gigantic for modern
commonwealth com

THE *BRIG-OF-WAR ØRNEN* WAS CLEARED FOR DEPARTURE FROM
ST. THOMAS ON DECEMBER 15, 1848, WITH GENERAL BUDDHOE
ON BOARD, WHERE IRMINGER LISTED NO SPECIFIC DESTINATION
BUT INSTEAD SUSPICIOUSLY JUST LISTED *"ISLANDS."*

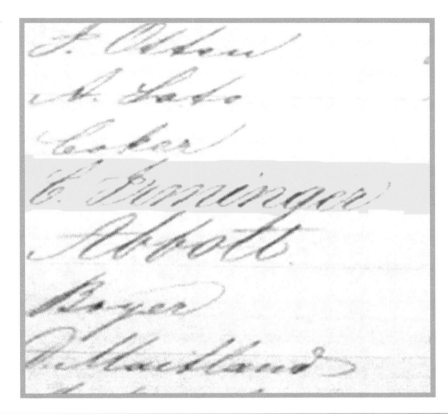

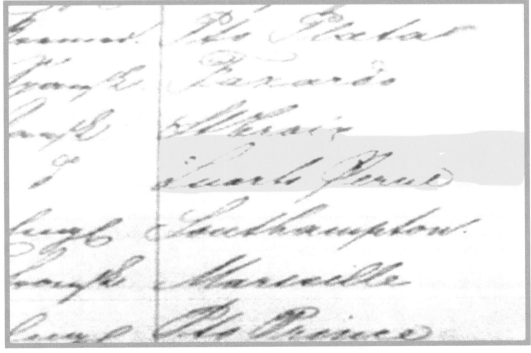

**CAPTAIN IRMINGER LISTING *"LAREDO, PERU"* ON ONE
OF THE DEPARTURE RECORDS FOR THE *ØRNEN*.**

CHAPTER XVIII

GOVERNOR-GENERAL PETER VON SCHOLTEN'S PERSONAL LETTERS

THIS CHAPTER CONTAINS A PHOTOGRAPH OF THE GOVERNOR-GENERAL Peter von Scholten and a few of his personal letters which he wrote to his childhood friend, Maria Eide, in 1852 in which he confessed that he and General Buddhoe worked collaboratively on the Emancipation and even had "a pact" in which they had made each other a promise.

It also contains a Memorandum written by W.R.J. Grant of a conversation he had with von Scholten in August of 1848. H.W. Petersen describes a conversation he had with von Scholten the day of and shortly following the Emancipation. There's also a letter written by von Scholten to his Attorney Liebenberg dated December 22, 1849 explaining, among other things, the atmosphere on the island and some the events leading up to the Emancipation.

Peter Carl Frederik von Scholten served as Governor-General of the Danish West Indies from 1827-1848. Von Scholten was born in Vestervig, Denmark on May 17, 1784 and died on January 26, 1854 in Altona, Holstein (present day Germany), just short of six years after the Emancipation, at the age of 69. He was buried in Copenhagen, Denmark. He was married to Anne Elisabeth Thorsten.

GOVERNOR-GENERAL PETER CARL FREDERIK von SCHOLTEN

MICH VRAA

FEMINA

JYLLANDS-POSTEN

POLITIKEN

★ ★ ★ ★ ★

FYENS STIFTSTIDENDE

ROMAN

PETERS KÆRLIGHED

„En ny generations vestindisk krønikeskriver."
JYLLANDS-POSTEN

**VESTINDIEN-TRILOGIEN
SOLGT I MERE END 50.000 EKSEMPLARER**

LINDHARDT OG RINGHOF

Peter's Love

On 14 July 1827, Peter von Scholten took office as Governor-General of Sankt Croix in the Danish West Indies.

Exactly twenty-one years later, on July 14, 1848, he left under the cover of darkness to sail to Denmark for the last time. Eleven days before, surrounded by many thousands of armed rebels and against the wishes of the Danish king and government, he had finally said the words that put an end to slavery in the Danish West Indies: Now you are free!

For twenty years, Peter von Scholten had shared table and bed with his great love, the coloured Anna Heegaard. After July 14, he never saw her again. The man who finally freed the Danes' slaves in 1848 was and remains a mystery.

How can one explain von Scholten's improbable lightning career from humble weighmaster in Charlotte Amalie at St. Thomas to the most powerful post in the Danish West Indies? Where did his close relationship with King Frederik VI come from, and why did the king fulfill all his wishes? And the greatest mystery of all: Did von Scholten secretly support the slaves in their final showdown with white supremacy.

"The Danes are cunning; they adapt. And now they're doing it again. Now they wash the blood from their hands; now they want to erase the memory of the hundreds of thousands whose lives they stole for their own gain. And then they will sail home and forget about us," from the book.

PETERS KÆRLIGHED follows HAABET, the first volume of Mich Vraa's trilogy of independent novels about the Danish slave trade.

We must think that in these last times he has let his eventful years slip past him in a variegated kaleidoscope and has sought to return to the islands where his heart was buried.

H. C. J. LAWAETZ, AUTHOR OF
"PETER von SCHOLTEN."

In essence what is more important in the end, the deeds of our life or the happiness of our youth or what we become in the end, the final stamp in the salmon seal of our reputation?

PETER von SCHOLTEN IN
LETTER TO MARIA EIDE

LETTERS: PETER von SCHOLTEN TO MARIA EIDE, COPENHAGEN AUGUST 1852

When I walk around the streets of Copenhagen today, I often feel that there are citizens who see me and think: There goes the traitor Scholten, the one who cost us the gold of our West Indian colonies. Once you've been blacked out, the dirt sticks. Truth and realities have a difficult time in the people's consciousness. And the writers would much rather slander than glorify.

As you know, I was finally acquitted by the Supreme Court only as recent as last April -- less than four months ago. It was compensation I got there, but the press hardly dealt with it, so that I am presumably still considered guilty in wide circles of the "laxity and lukewarmness" for which the commission court sentenced me a good year before.

For more than a year I carried around this date: that I had failed the West Indies and Denmark and the Danish King by not dealing brutally with the rebellious negroes on that July day in 1848.

The original accusations that I was in league with the Negro leaders -- first of all with John Gottlieb Buddo -- I was admittedly not convicted, but the suspicion remained. And, as mentioned, the acquittal in the Supreme Court has not changed that. People remember the stories of how John rode with me to the plantations during the last hard time and helped calm the negroes. Many called him teasing "Scholten's right hand."

You remember John Buddo, I know. This deeply honorable man whom Anna introduced me to in 1841. That evening in July he did his best to prevent blood from flowing through the streets of Frederiksted. Today, I dare to admit that there was a pact between Buddo and me. We had made each other a promise. He was to ensure that no whites were harmed, and I had to let the negroes assemble in Frederiksted without deploying the military. That is why we sailed that day to Christiansted instead of Frederiksted; therefore, I hesitated so long before setting out for the West End. When I finally arrived on the afternoon of July 3rd, the demand for freedom was too strong. The fire had taken hold and could no longer be put out!

There was only one way to go - to set them free - and it was I who said the words that day -- forty-four years after I first set foot on West Indian soil.

Monday, 16 August 1852

Dear Maria:

Why is it, Maria, that when you look back on your life's adventures, the memories are probably golden and desirable, but in a strange way, not as precious as you would like to imagine. It is now even more possible to enjoy something that has passed, with the same strength that one can rejoice over what lies ahead. Or even what is now, right now.

I have always, I think, been good to the last. I have lived. God knows I have. I have loved, yes. I have achieved everything I set out to do. And yet...

I think so often of you and your husband and the great help you were when my strength failed me at the very end. No one could wish for a truer friend, and I miss you dearly and hope you are well. It's now summer, but in this country summer is a rather pale affair compared to even the Christmas weather in the West Indies. Although I know I have often sighed about the heat, I also miss it. My old bones is not made for cold and wind.

Old, yes, I am old. My health is not good, but after the judgment of the Supreme Court and the compensation I received therefrom, I have gotten a little better. There are actually days now when for short periods I feel almost comfortable.

Earlier this year, I bought a nice little property on Kongens Nytorv, right by the main gate. There are only three floors and a dormer, but I have arranged myself quite nicely, and I have actually started holding small parties again. If anyone still calls me "Prince Peter" it happens behind my back. After the recovery, I experienced the most kindness from my circle of friends; and in any case I am more "Peter" than I am "prince" these days.

Even though I thus live fairly well, and am not exactly lonely, I can still feel that the memories are intruding. It is probably a natural consequence of aging. But as I wrote in my introduction, memories cannot measure up to the joy of the moment, life as it is lived in this very moment.

They are just so obscenely lifelike -- these memories. Faces, places, smells, all lining up to step into an old man's dreams.

Even here, almost exactly half a century after I first saw the knobbly profiles of the islands in the Caribbean Sea, I can hear the anchor chain piling out through the cleat under the deck of the brig at the very hour of day when I docked in Charlotte Amalie for the very first time. And I remember the sight of the red tilted roofs of the bright buildings under the winding sun in front of the mountain massif.

On the ridge above the city were larger properties the mansions on Kommandantbakken, from where the view is so indescribably beautiful, and where the sea breeze brings a bit of coolness to the luckiest residents of the hot city.

It was the 13th of August. I had just turned twenty years old, and I think I can say, without being guilty of any exaggeration, that no more adventurous lad had set out into the world that year from King's Copenhagen. My journey to the distant West Indies had certainly not come about at my instigation, but along the way I had heard so many stories.

It was my father, the commandant on Sankt Thomas, who had commanded that I travel there with him. One day he came riding alone at the National Cadet Academy in Bredgade at home in Copenhagen, steered his horse inside the wall and strode across the square towards the corner where I happened to be in the company of a few other cadets.

"Sheep!" I shouted when I saw him. I was relieved to see him safe and sound after our long separation. There is no telling what the sojourn in the tropics and the thousands of nautical miles on the ocean can do to a man, not least one of his age. My father, Casimir von Scholten, had reached fifty and had tried more than most men, for a short year he was an English prisoner of war, and he had only returned to the command house in Charlotte Amalie the previous year.

"Is it the young Ensign Peter Scholten?" sounded his words with the mixture of severity and pointed whim which was his characteristic. The truth was that I should have finished cadet training a long time ago, but I had honestly never felt that it was so urgent.

"Like," I replied, quickly changing the subject. "How nice to see you, Dad," I said smiling my truest smile. "How has your journey gone? And you must tell me the latest news from the West Indies. Is prosperity still flourishing after the English occupation?"

My father grumbled and brushed some dust off his coat rack. I could see that he had grown older. His hair was more white than gray now, but there was a twinkle in his eyes. He always had a sly look in them, and behind his high forehead lived an extremely sharp brain.

Now you might think I'm forgetting that you yourself have met my father, Maria, but that is by no means the case. I remember your poignancy quite well and the account of the time the Frigate Haabet was wrecked, and you spoke to him in Christiansfort, fifteen years old and wearing only the commander's own freshly ironed nightshirt. And although it's not polite to point out a woman's age, it strikes me that if I'm old, you are not that much younger! However, I trust that you are still as adorable as you were. You have mysteriously never let the passing of the years trouble you.

Another memory comes from the time many years later when you returned to the islands at Christmas time on your father's brigantine. Back then I didn't know you yet, but I did know a little about Mikkel who introduced us to each other. I immediately saw how in love he was, and I must confess that I sometimes think about what might have happened between us if his love had not been so obvious to everyone. Have I ever confessed to you, Maria, how easily I could have fallen in love then?

That time - just as you had arrived - was my last in Charlotte Amalie. I sailed to Denmark, and when I returned fifteen months later, it was to the island where you spent most of your youth. Fate made it so that we switched places; you came to Saint Thomas and I came to Saint Croix. As Governor General, no less. It felt like a glorious victory. A triumph in just twelve years, the humble weighmaster had reached the highest post in the West Indies.

~~~~#~~~~

Wednesday, 18 August 1852

Dearest Maria:

I have occasionally toyed with the idea of writing my memoirs. I have been told that the brave Admiral Birch Dahlerup, whom I have known most of my life, and whom I dare to call my friend, is engaged in writing some very extensive memoirs, which he hopes to finish before he leaves this world. But Dahlerup is a man with so many orders and distinctions that it is surprising that his dress chest can carry all that metal; and he has also lived quite an adventurous, eventful life where mine almost pales in comparison.

However, I mostly stayed in the West Indies, while Dahlerup sailed all the world's oceans and ended his tumultuous career as Commander-in-Chief of the Austro-Hungarian Navy. While I merely steered three little islands into freedom! And then it strikes me that the haste that is said to characterize Dahlerup's work might just be timely. He is six years younger than me and of course in much better health, so the risk that I would scratch before I reached the third canitel is quite imminent.

~~~~#~~~~

ANNALY BAY TIDE POOLS

SUGARCANE FIELD LABORERS – ST. CROIX

Memorandum of remarks made by Governor General von Scholten in London to W.R.J. Grant - August 1848

He knew very well that as soon as he heard of the insurrection at Martinique that the same thing will happen on St. Croix.

He was very sorry for Grant, Buchby, Tower and Christmas. Newton was rich enough in this country. And as for those Irish fellows who had made their fortunes in St. Croix and bought estates, he did not care a damn for them. [Danish word: Skidton/Skidtom or Skidtem] meaning in English "Shitty!" What would they do now?

He said it was his opinion the government at home would be very glad at what had happened.

He said he had not emancipated the negroes, that they had taken it themselves and that therefore it was his opinion the King was absolved from any responsibility as regards compensation.

He asked Mr. Grant, who he thought was best adapted to be Governor of the island -- a man who had estates, or one who was independent of the island? Mr. Grant thought that a person having an interest in the island was preferable. "Oh then, he answered, you prefer Oxholm to me?"

He said if this King would give him a Frigate and 300 soldiers, he thought he would go out again.

He shouts -- recommends that the Planters give the negroes provision grounds for that would encourage them to stay on the properties.

~~~~#~~~~

H.W. Petersen, Royal Cashier, Captain of Militia Hunter Corps

[This examination took place 10 January 1849]

After that, **H.W. Petersen, Royal Cashier, Captain for the Militia Hunter Corps,** appeared, explaining that he, before the riot broke out, did not have the faintest idea that such things could be going on, and until 8 o'clock Monday morning he did not know anything about what was going on.

As he, at the mentioned time, from a woman neighbor in his home, had heard what had been going on in the night, he went down to the Government House, and on the way, he met the Commanding Sergeant of the mentioned Hunter Corps, who had been ordered to notify some of the crew to be ready for moving out.

When the person questioned arrived in the Government House, he found some persons present by General Scholten, talking about that the General should go to the West End. However, some – the person questioned does not remember who – advised the General not to go there, as they presumed that the negroes possibly might seize the General's person, so much more as his carriage on his way here from Frederiksted had been stopped.

During the conversation the General asked the persons present, what he should say to the negroes when he met them, to which the person questioned, as nobody else answered to this, remarked that it was right for the General to warn them to be quiet, as in the opposite case strict precautions would be taken. The person questioned remarks that he himself at that time had temporarily left active service at the Hunter Corps, and because of that no order as to this could be given him, but such an order had been given to his brother, who is Premier Lieutenant at the Corps. But on occasion of the riots that had broken out the person questioned himself now took the command. After that, Colonel de Nully and Lieutenant Meincke had been sent to Frederiksted, the person questioned left the Government House that morning.

He talked to General Scholten both Monday evening, as the General returned from Frederiksted, and some time Tuesday and Wednesday, but as the General did not tell him his thoughts as to what had happened, or what he on this occasion would do, the person questioned reassures that he does not know anything about the motives having led General Scholten at his various activities on occasion of the riot, and also the person questioned does not know anything about where the uprising had started and what had started it.

That it should have been the General's intention to emancipate the negroes when he came to Frederiksted, he has not in any way hinted to the person questioned, and the person questioned had never heard that it should be the General's intention at the first given opportunity to emancipate the black people.

During the days after the riot the person questioned held his post in this city, where he inspected the various guard posts, sometimes together with the General himself.

On the Tuesday, the General arranged for the dissemination of the Proclamation about the emancipation, and he also had told the Catholic and the English vicar to go out into the country, for by the reasons of the religion, to try to influence the restless population. And, on the whole, as far as the person questioned knows, the General's intention was by mild means to influence the mood among the blacks.

Tuesday in the morning the person questioned went to the Custom House, where he saw General Scholten on horseback, surrounded by a lot of people (the volunteers from St. Thomas had landed at the same time). He noticed that a few of the persons present talked with vehemence to the General, but the person questioned could not hear what it was about.

Shortly after, the person questioned appeared in the Government House, where he met him, together with Councillor of Justice Fæster, and they were talking together. It seemed to be somewhat vehement, but the person questioned cannot say what they were talking about, as the person questioned had his attention drawn to the General, who looked suffering, and suddenly he saw the General sinking down on the sofa, saying to the person questioned that he must go to get Colonel de Nully and Major Falbe, which the person questioned immediately did, Councillor of Justice Fæster following him.

The person questioned brought the two-mentioned gentlemen back to the General, who now asked them to take over the military command, as he had got ill. The person questioned has not heard General Scholten use the words mentioned by Colonel de Nully about the command, which was decided that day to send out against the negroes. Because of that he assumes that he at that time when the words were used, he was not at all present. The person questioned is convinced that the order to send out the detachment on the Thursday has gone out from the General himself, but now he cannot say from where he has this knowledge.

When de Nully and Falbe had left, the General was, by the person questioned, together with the servant, brought up into his bedroom and to his bed. He was then extremely debunked and unconscious. Because of that there was sent for Doctor Ruan and maybe at the same time for Doctor Knudsen, who earlier had attended the General.

The doctors prohibited everybody going to see the General, and the person questioned knows that the written order that was published to the military commanders-in-chief, was not signed the day when it was dated.

Just from the time when the riot broke out the General had complained to the person questioned that he felt unwell, and especially that he could not sleep at night; but he had been fully conscious until he, as remarked, the above-mentioned morning fell back in the sofa.

It seems to the person questioned that he that Thursday morning (6 July), when the General was brought to his bed, that the person questioned saw the Government Councillor Kunzen outside the General's bedroom, but seeing in which condition the General was, Government Councillor Kunzen went away without talking to him.

What was decided by General Scholten as to the Civil Board, the person questioned does not know, and he was not present at the negotiations that took place on occasion of the Government Commission's meeting, and neither did he participate in the undertakings of the same, neither has he been in touch with the mentioned commission, and neither has he received any orders from it.

Friday 7th July, the Interim Councillor of Government, Councillor of the Chancellery Petersen appeared by the person questioned, expressing the wish of speaking to the General. He followed the person questioned after that the General had been prepared for that visit. Both Councillor of the Chancellery Petersen and Councillor of the Government Kunzen went to the General, informing him of the fact that in the West End the Government

Commission was not recognized. Because of that, the General expressed that it might be best that his brother and Procurator Sarauw were assigned to the commission to avoid dissatisfaction at the West End.

It seems to the person questioned that the General on this occasion was asked whether it was with his consent that the commission had gathered, to which the General answered in the affirmative, but at that time he was very frail, though the person questioned thinks that he was by full sense.

Later the person questioned was summoned, and as the person questioned alerted him to the fact that the meetings of the Government Commission had aroused general displeasure, and he advised him to summon Chamberlain Oxholm from St. Thomas to give him the command. The General decided to do so, and order as to this was sent to Oxholm.

During the following days the General stayed in his rooms, and although it seemed that he became a little better, he still was very frail, until 14th July he left the country.

The person questioned assumes that if force had been used against the negroes immediately at the beginning at the West End, the riot possibly could have been stifled at the beginning, but he dared not express any definite opinion about this, so much less that one could not know immediately if the riot had spread.

The person questioned does not know and does not assume that any force had been used to General Scholten to make him put down the command, but it cannot be denied that the mood was against him, both from the part of the Planters and from the part of the Managers. The person questioned assumes that the state of his health made it inevitable to abolish the high command.

~~~~#~~~~

VISIT OF PRINCE VALDEMAR OF DENMARK TO ST. CROIX - 1879

LETTER BY PETER von SCHOLTEN TO HIS ATTORNEY LIEBENBERG, DATED DECEMBER 22, 1849.

Peter von Scholtens forklaring pa oproret i 1848 og ophrevelsen af slaveriet (1849)

Kildeteksten er Peter von Scholtens brev ti/ sin advokat, Liebenberg, den 22. december 1849. Brevet blev skrevet i forbindelse med den retssag, der efterfulgte .frigivelsen af slaverne i Dansk Vestindien den 3. juli 1848. Brevet er oprindeligt skrev!t p.A¥ dansk, menjindes her i engelsk oversA:ttelse (oversat af Eva Lawaetz). Originalbrevet ligger pA¥ Rigsarkivet i KA.benhavn.

Fra Eva Lawaetz (red): Emancipation in the Danish West Indies: Eyewitness Accounts II. *St. Croix: VDCCA, Bureau of Libraries, Museums and Archaeological Services, 1973.*

Previously I have forwarded to Your Honor a number of documents and papers that might be helpful in clarifying the situation for you. At the same time, I want to let you know the confidence and trust I have in your handling of my case in the best possible way. I am enclosing more documents for your information according to the attached list. At the same time, I am handing you the following notations for your possible use or guidance in this case.

It will only be possible to understand my action on July 3, 1848 in St. Croix when the negro insurrection took place, and to pass a fair and just judgment of the necessity of the Proclamation of the Emancipation, when the atmosphere in the colonies and my situation as Governor-General are taken into consideration.

First, it must be remembered that after the Royal Proclamation of July 28, 1847, all children born to the unfree after the issuance of this proclamation would be free at birth, while the same Royal decree dictated that a period of 12 years of transition should exist for the unfree. This was bound to cause a difficult and precarious situation, not only among the Planters, but the slaves, who, of course, had a stronger demand for freedom because it now had been promised within not too many years.

It is a well-known fact that the Planters were not pleased with the decree of July 28, 1847 providing for the freedom of all children born after that date and promising final Emancipation at a certain stipulated time.

The slaves did not want to wait 12 years for Emancipation and constantly complained about the treatment of their free children. On the other hand, it was quite natural that the Planters now neglected the children; they were considered a burden because the Planters could not be compensated through the children who work on the plantation when they grew up.

As a matter of fact, on every holiday after the proclamation of the Royal Decree, a number of mothers complained to me about the Planters' treatment of their children.

Thus, the situation became more complicated in the colonies and it was more difficult to preserve the status quo. It must also be remembered that, during the year after the proclamation of the British emancipation (1833) conditions have been dangerous and not very reassuring. All the slaves longed for Emancipation, without understanding its real impact on every-day life and individual well-being. Add to this the new development in the French colonies, which complicated the situation even more.

It is commonly felt that the Emancipation in the French colonies was a consequence of the French Revolution in 1848, which caused a change in the form of government and the constitution.

About the same time, or shortly thereafter, it came to the attention of the slaves in our islands that the Danish Constitution had been changed, but of course they did not know anything about the importance and the consequences of this change so far as the Danish West Indies were concerned. But anybody who has lived in our colonies will understand that the slaves in our islands generally would believe that, just as the change in the French Constitution had brought Emancipation to their brothers in the French colonies, a change in the Danish Constitution would result in theirs. As a matter of fact, many slaves were so sure of their Emancipation that they believed the proclamation to be arbitrarily delayed.

The fact that the slaves knew about the revolution in France in February and in Denmark in March had severe consequences for the whole situation in the Danish Islands. Even the sober, quiet, better part of the slaves came to look at an insurrection and/or a strong demand for freedom in quite another way.

In an uprising, the leaders could calculate on support in a violent demonstration even from those who were not dissatisfied with their conditions of life. Because the leaders could expect general support from the slave population, the outbreak of an uprising would be in their control.

It is well documented that the principal provision in the Decree of July 28, 1847, that is, the freedom of the slave children, was not engineered by me or anybody else connected with the government in the Danish West Indies. On the contrary, both in writing and by words of mouth, I seriously objected to it. I even openly explained, and without reservation to His Majesty King Christian VIII, that the situation caused by this gradual emancipation could not be controlled. I could even refer to a conversation with His Majesty the King, who, in reply to my remonstrances, answered that the Emancipation has to be granted, if necessary, and I (the King) am willing to give you the necessary authority to act in order not to subject either the country or the whites to the disaster of revolution.

But to this I objected that neither for the King's sake nor for my own did I want to have this authority. Such an authority could easily give rise to prompt claims for compensation when the Emancipation was going to become a reality. Such authority could not be kept a secret from the Planters, and they would become even more suspicious of me than before; as if I had wanted to have the power as soon as possible to proclaim final Emancipation.

Rather, all my endeavours have been concentrated on slowly and systematically, through education, to prepare the free coloured and the slaves for their rights and obligations as citizens and for their freedom.

It is also very important to understand my position as Governor- General of the Danish West Indies, and to remember that the military force in the islands was negligible, far from sufficient to suppress an ordinary uprising. Nothing could be done about this because the presence of a sufficient military force on the islands would have involved exorbitant expense. Therefore, I have never suggested using these means to safeguard the colonies against uprising or to secure general quiet and order. I have always directed my efforts toward creating a well-organized police force and towards improving the conditions for the Negroes, especially their morality, because in my opinion, this provides the best guarantee for maintaining a quiet life and continued development in the colonies.

Even in more recent times, the police were far from being in proper shape. However, I cannot be blamed for that, because for many years I have repeatedly requested an in-depth reorganization of the police in the islands. But my recommendations have not been followed, whereas measures I strongly opposed have been adopted.

For your information, I will just mention that, against the strong opposition stated in my proposal of April 30, 1840, the white and free-coloured police in St. Croix were exempted from night duty, and thus also from night patrols.

Speaking about the morality of the Negroes, I certainly appreciate the efforts made by the government. I do hope my efforts will also be remembered. However, many things have not been done or even attempted; much has been left undone, in spite of my recommendations and hard work to realize my aims.

I will not elaborate on all the difficulties with the Planters whenever I tried to improve the conditions of the slaves, especially after the Emancipation of the free-coloured. I will only mention those situations that have been impossible for me to correct by means of proposals to the government in Denmark or efforts in the colonies. This has had a very dangerous impact on the Negro population.

First, I want to mention the testimony of slaves in court. Although, educationally speaking, they should qualify as witnesses, very special and very complicated rules govern their right to testify. Because of this I have often been compelled (against my moral conviction) to dismiss a case, or, when the owners, managers or overseers, with very few exceptions, insisted that their word could be trusted, however far from the truth.

Even more damaging for the morality of the Negro population was the fact that the managers and overseers pursued young Negro girls. They often promised the girls' own mother that they would buy freedom for the girl and the children she might bear. In this way they succeeded in persuading young girls to live with them; but later on they could not be induced to honor this solemn promise.

In this connection, I want to mention that a manager on the Enfield Green Plantation near Frederiksted had in this way persuaded a girl, hardly fourteen years old, to live with him in his house. After he had three children by her, he let both the girl and the children remain slaves, disregarding all remonstrances from the owner and from the Governor-General. He could do this without punishment because there did not exist any law, nor could one be passed, forbidding that kind of seduction. I could not even obtain an oath on the Holy Bible that he disclaimed to be the father of the children. A free man's word against a slave was sufficient.

Such behaviour can have the most terrible consequences. Almost at the same time on the plantation, the manager and the overseer were killed by poisoning. The overseer lived with the daughter of an old mulatto woman. He had promised to buy the freedom of the daughter and the children, if any. He did have a child by her, but for a long time he had refused to buy their freedom, making all kinds of excuses. The mother had her revenge by putting instant plant poison in his coffee, killing not only him, but also another completely innocent victim.

The morality of the Negro population and my ability to carry out orders suffered when my efforts to improve conditions were not supported by government. The government's failure to support me had the most unfortunate influence on my authority and, in the colonies, this is one of the worst things that can happen.

If you consider the colonies from a European point of view, it will scarcely be possible to understand the moral damage suffered when the Governor-General's authority was not supported, but often undermined by the government in Denmark. Everybody familiar with life in the colonies, and who is able and willing to consider the importance of their peculiarities, has to admit I am right.

To illustrate what I mean, I will just point out that the Governor-General over a long period of time had to suffer at the hands of an inferior official in the islands who was allowed to write and behave in a spiteful manner toward the island's highest authority without any interference from the government, at the very time when his authority needed support more than ever. This was bound to weaken and diminish that authority, paralyse his strength, and damage the situation which after so much work and difficulty, was nearing a happy solution without any disruption in the conditions of life or any considerable increase in expenses.

Finally, this official was found guilty and sentenced to pay a fine, but because of his insulting remarks about the Governor-General, it was necessary for me to bring another action against him. But this time, the government reinstated him in office instead of suspending him as in the first case.

This was a very unfortunate decision, the more so because my efforts to settle conditions in the colonies; to maintain the rights of the free-coloured, and to improve conditions of life for the slaves, were bound to evoke.the Planter's opposition. Even if such opposition was not shown openly very often, it was always alive and directed toward damaging any position as Governor-General. Therefore, I needed all possible moral support from the government.

The radical changes in several military and civil branches of the administration which I proposed and carried out, especially within the administration of the Royal Plantations, injured many private interests as the Royal Exchequer improved. Of course, this was fuel to the fire of opposition.

This, then, was the situation when the insurrection broke out, and therefore the instigators almost succeeded in keeping it secret.

In my letter of September 25, 1848, concerning the first questions, I have intimated that there were no indications of an uprising in the near future. But I also pointed out, that in an apparently quiet situation, extraordinary measures can never be kept a secret from the Negro population and will cause extreme tension in the population who will try to find out the reason why such measures have been introduced. They will conclude that the government is afraid of an uprising and has realized their power. In this way the measures taken to prevent an uprising might easily become the reason for one.

But as the court hearings in the colonies have been finished by now, we will know if anybody in the colonies knew anything about the outbreak of a rebellion, and if there is any reason to blame me for lack of vision or less foresight than others.

Whether I should have crushed the revolt at birth with the force I used to subdue the rebellion after the proclamation of the Emancipation has been answered in the previously mentioned letter of September 25th, question six.

It makes a great difference if you deal with the whole population. The more sensible and reasonable segment, due to events in Denmark in March 1848, believed their cause to be justified and reasonable and a common cause for the whole population rather than with a malicious, thoughtless and shameless crowd that would make much greater demands than would the reasonable element whose support they will thus lose.

At that time not a single man, not one single voice suggested the use of force, thus provoking unspeakable grief without solving the problem. The history of the French colonies during the first revolution was a dire warning to everybody, and at that time there was a comparatively stronger military force in Martinique than in St. Croix in 1848.

And I am sure that if it had been possible to call the Planters together and ask for their opinion, the more sensible and realistic of them would have advised me to do exactly what I did. Today, when their properties and lives are not in any danger, it is only natural that they should have another opinion because the only way they can expect to obtain any compensation is to maintain that it was not necessary to emancipate the slaves and therefore they suffered unnecessary losses.

There are two more things I want to point out, even if they are not legal proof; however, they ought to be considered when deciding whether I have proclaimed Emancipation without any need or reason.

In the first place, I have never supported a suddenly proclaimed Emancipation. On the contrary, all my work as Governor and Governor- General proves that I considered that an Emancipation had to be prepared gradually to qualify the Negro population for the conditions of freedom. Because of this, I have been attacked so many times, both at home and abroad, and therefore am entitled to believe that I am not an 'Emancipist' in the general meaning of the word.

Is there any reason to expect me suddenly to have proclaimed an Emancipation that was not absolutely necessary? I did not have any property in the islands to be concerned about. Should I suddenly have changed my lifelong attitude, if it had not been necessary? And should I have preferred to proclaim an Emancipation so evidently against my plans, the work of my whole life? Furthermore, I had worked successfully in the realization of my plans.

Consider the quiet and orderly conditions in the colonies since the slaves have been emancipated for these past 18 months. Compare them with conditions in the colonies of other countries where a sudden Emancipation has either been given or taken. Doesn't it show that generally speaking, my administration policy and efforts were appropriate, considering the conditions in the colonies?

Today, others might admit against their will, that my work for the benefit of the colonies had been very fruitful, and will continue to be, therefore, why should I hesitate to admit it myself? Sudden Emancipation will bring more dangers and less real advantages to the black population whose happiness and civilization has meant so much to me during so many years and have been the object and aim of all my activity.

I have thought it wise to send you these notes and presentations and, at the same time, I once more assure you of my unlimited respect and trust in you.

RUINS AT FORMER MT. VICTORY SCHOOL

CHAPTER XIX

ANNA ELIZABETH ULRICKA HEEGAARD

THIS SECTION CONTAINS A PHOTOGRAPH OF ANNA HEEGAARD AND OF *Bülowsminde* (the home shared by Heegaard von Scholten) in Christiansted. It also contains a list of Anna Heegaard's 15 slaves by name. These slaves worked at a place called *"Hafensight"* (a plot of land within *Bülowsminde*). Also attached here is a photograph of her grave stone.

We learned from our research that Bülowsminde was bought in 1834. Von Scholten named it in memory of the "Adjutant-General Bülow," who in Denmark had made a profitable connection with King Frederik VI and himself possible. *"Minde"* in the Danish language means "memory of." Heegaard seemed to have influenced von Scholten to give better treatment and favor to the "free-coloureds," but not the general slave population. She made absolutely no such intercessions for the enslaved.

There's also a translation and excerpt showing that at least five of Heegaard's slaves were children. There's also a historical biography of Anna Heegaard's life in a paper entitled "History Corner" by Isidore Paiewonsky.

Anna Heegaard was born on St. Croix on January 28, 1790 and died on January 1, 1859 at the age of 68. She was buried at No. 40 Estate Aldershville in Christiansted.

ANNA ELIZABETH ULRICKA HEEGAARD

H. W. Petersen

[This examination took place 10 January 1849]

The person questioned here is Royal Treasurer, Captain of the Hunter Corps of the Militia and Curator to Miss Heegaard, H.W. Petersen.

The person questioned is Curator to General Scholten's previous housekeeper, Miss Heegaard, and intimately familiar with her affairs. Thus, he knows for certain that she for several years before the Emancipation has only possessed the following slaves, which can be proved by means of the tax lists: John, Robert, Johannes (with the surname Bitters) Peter, Eliza and the boys Julius and Augustus.

Of these, Johannes, according to petition from Captain Christmas to the Royal Department Liquidation Commission of 28 May last year, was sold to the Royal Plantation Sion Farm, which Christmas is managing. From this petition, which the person questioned produced, it can be seen that this negro for more than two years had been leased to Christmas to work as a carpenter at the mentioned plantation. And Augustus was, almost at the same time, traded away to Christmas for a woman negro Maria, who, as well as the other above- mentioned slaves, except for Johannes, was still owned by Miss Heegaard when the Emancipation was given, and so became free.

The person questioned is of the opinion that from this, it is clear that there is no basis for the rumor that Miss Heegaard, a short time before the riot, had sold her slaves, adding that in the year of 1848 she has much more increased their numbers, having bought a woman negro named Sally with two children from Planter Skelton at Canaan.

Those three slaves were still owned by her, together with the above- mentioned, when the Emancipation was given.

~~~~#~~~~

[This examination took place 11 January 1849]

It was remarked that Captain and Cashier Petersen to-day has produced the signing person a receipt, issued by C. Skelton, according to which Miss Heegaard 10 April last year has bought the negro woman Sally with 2 children, Frederik and Charlotte, from C. Skelton, paying 128 dollars for them.

~~~~#~~~~

[This examination took place 22nd January 1849]

> Finally a receipt was produced and is quoted under No. 33. According to this, Miss Heegaard, at the end of the year of 1847, had paid "head tax" for 7 negroes. Also it was noticed that there has not been paid any "head tax".
> The attachment No. 33 reads as follows:

No. 33

The country house Hafensight

Mrs. Heegaard has today paid into the land fund "head tax" for 1847 of seven negroes with 7 Rigsdaler Danish currency, for which hereby receipt is given."

St. Croix
The Citizen Council's Cashier's Office
25 November 1847

Noted: W. Simmiolkjier

Keutsch

[Produced during the examination 22nd January 1849].

Flensborg

[After this the examination was postponed].

<div align="center">~~~~#~~~~</div>

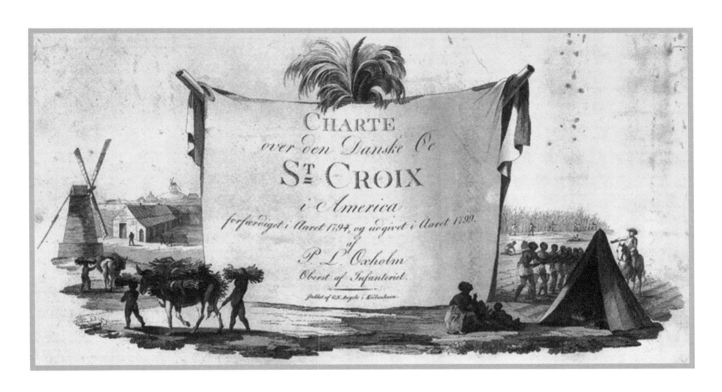

On this cartouche from Peter Lotharius Oxholm's map of St. Croix, published in 1799, two groups of enslaved children are seen. Both the small children, who were being watched over at the edge of the field while the parents worked (at right) and the older children, who helped with driving the mules home (at left). Danish National Archives, Rentekammeret ("Chamber of Revenue "), Archive No. 303, Kort og tegninger ("Maps and drawings") 1600-1920, Map No. 337.007.

LIST OF ANNA HEEGAARD'S SLAVES

1. John

2. Robert

3. Johannes "Bitters"

4. Peter

5. Malvina

6. Eliza

7. Julius**

8. Augustus**

9. Sally

10. Frederik**

11. Charlotte**

12. Maria

13. Caesar

14. Justus

15. Emelie**

** = [Enslaved Children]

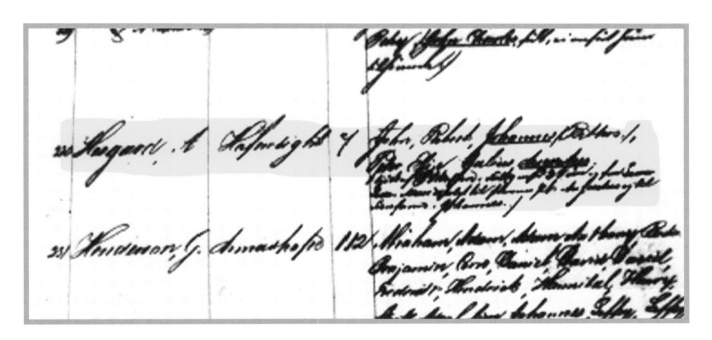

AN INVENTORY OF ANNA HEEGAARD'S SLAVES ON "HAFENSIGHT" (A PLOT OF LAND WITHIN *BÜLOWSMINDE)*, AT WHICH TIME SHE LISTED (7) SLAVES. HOWEVER, SHE BOUGHT ADDITIONAL SLAVES IN THE SPRING OF 1848 JUST PRIOR TO EMANCIPATION.

Anna Elizabeth Heegaard

B6	
Type	Images
Description	Daguerreotype in airtight frame with glass by Anna Ulricka Elisabeth Heegaard (1790-1859), Governor-General Peter von Scholten's light-coloured partner at the country house Biilowsminde just outside Christiansted on St. Croix. She lived in her own home "Havensight" on Billowsminde. Her mother was Susanna Uytendahl, a mulatto and domestic slave in Christiansted, St. Croix until her 12th birthday.
Remark	A similar specimen, but mirrored, exists. Today, the two daguerreotypes are owned by Anna Heegaard's family members. Benoni James Petersen (1848-1930) has in his memoirs of his childhood on St. Croix told the following about his aunt Anna Heegaard: "Mrs. Heegaard had for many years managed Biilowsminde and represented at the great parties that Peter von Scholten gave in the period from the end of 1820 until 1848. He appreciated her very much, and she was a lady who conducted herself with much devotion and was very well regarded. In 1848, the Scholthenian glory ceased due to the Negro uprising and his resignation. Peter von Scholten left it all and went home, dying on January 26, 1854 in Altona. The place and the other glories were shared, and the many things scattered around, but there was a lot left for Mrs. Heegaard. The property was sold and bought by Mrs. Heegaard, and there were still many beautiful things up there on "Bakken", as we called it, and of which some things are still in my possession." Benoni James Petersen continues: "On Mondays, a certain bell regularly came to her carriage and stopped outside the door of my parents' house in Christiansted. She was going to town in business; She brought for us freshly baked cakes - do bread, - fruits, etc."
Period	1830 - 1859

BÜLOWSMINDE – **FRONTAL VIEW**

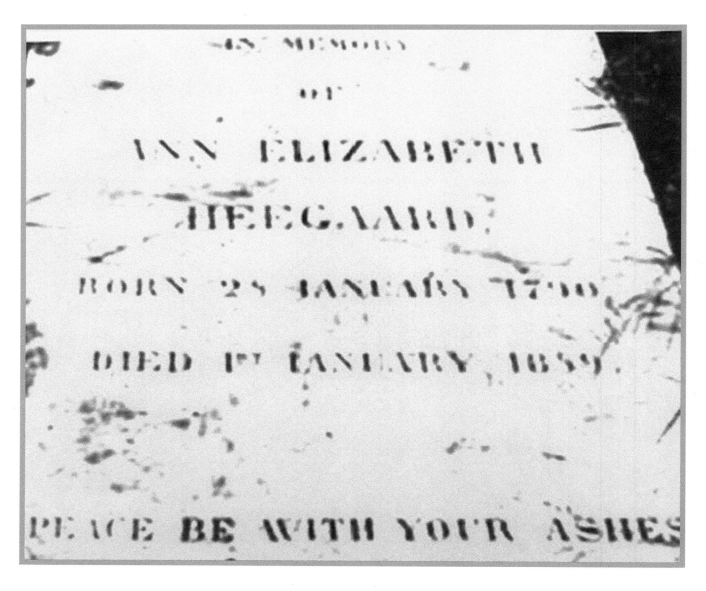

IN MEMORY

OF

ANN ELIZABETH

HEEGAARD,

BORN 28 JANUARY 1790

DIED 1ST JANUARY 1859.

PEACE BE WITH YOUR ASHES

**ANNA HEEGAARD'S GRAVE STONE, UPON WHICH IS
WRITTEN *"PEACE BE WITH YOUR ASHES."***

ANNA HEEGAARD, Grave #40-C "Johannes Ludwig Wittrog was buried in the
grounds of his estate, "Aldershville", here, too, lies his step-sister ANNA HEEGAARD.
His tomb has been obliterated in the years passed: hence his Danish descendants
had this bronze plague mounted on the grave of his spouse in AD 1966. RIP".

Anna Heegaard, Mistress of Governor General Peter von Scholten

from "History Corner" by Isidore Paiewonsky
Reprinted with permission from the family of Isidore Paiewonsky February 23,1976

Anna Elizabeth Ulricka Heegaard, the future mistress and consort of Peter von Scholten, was born in St. Croix during the early days of January, 1790. Approximately one month later, February 14, 1790, she was christened in a Negro church in Christiansted.

The baptismal record lists her father as Jacob Heegaard, white, native of Denmark, birthplace: Copenhagen, 1761. Her mother is listed as a "free mulatto woman," Susanna Uytendahl, born in St. Croix, in 1774. Jacob Heegaard, a member of a middle-class mercantile family in Copenhagen, came to the islands in a minor capacity as Government Clerk. He worked his way up the colonial bureaucracy until he attained the post as Treasurer of Customs, Christiansted. His relationship with Susanna Uytendahl must have been a casual sexual one leading to an undesired pregnancy on his part, for 2 weeks before Anna Elizabeth was christened, Heegaard blatantly ignored his relationship with the Uytendahl mulatto woman and his newly born child and married a white woman in Christiansted.

Left on her own, Susanna, raised Heegaard's child with the help of her mother. The records indicate that at the age of 14, on July 8, 1804, Anna was confirmed in the Lutheran Church, Christiansted. She was listed as a one-fourth coloured person.

Susanna Uytendahl's financial and domestic difficulties were eased somewhat when she entered into a common law relationship with an amiable retired sea captain, Hans Cappel. She bore him two daughters before he died in 1798.

Next, Susanna lived with a Danish shopkeeper and widower, Peter Abraham Wittrog, in a relationship that endured for 10 years. During this period, Susanna bore Wittrog a son. By all indications, Anna Heegaard got along well with her half-brother and her 2 half-sisters. Throughout her mother's relationships, Anna was reared and accepted as a member of the particular family in which she found herself. She grew into an attractive, confident and self-reliant person.

At the age of 19, Anna Heegaard began a series of relationships of her own. She attracted the attention of a 26-year old unmarried Danish attorney, Christopher Hansen, and she became his mistress.

Hansen made it clear to her from the beginning that his stay in the islands was not permanent. In the event that Anna should conceive a child by him, financial provisions would be made for the proper support and upbringing of that child. However, no offspring resulted from the relationship, which lasted a little more than four years.

In 1814, Anna Heegaard became involved with an Irishman, Paul Twigg. He had come to the islands from Dublin in 1810, at the age of 28. He went into business in Christiansted and was quite successful. Dahlerup, the Danish sea captain and historian, who knew Twigg, described him as "a very sociable and jovial man, who loved to entertain."

Evidently unmarried, Twigg looked around for a good housekeeper and hostess to help him with his household duties and his numerous parties. Anna had been recommended to him as having the necessary qualifications. After meeting Miss Heegaard and being pleasantly impressed, Twigg invited her to join his household and to take over.

Whatever the relationship with Twigg was, it could not have been too binding, for it is recorded that from 1816-1820, Anna Heegaard lived with her mother, Susanna Uytendahl, in Susanna's house in Compagnigade, Christiansted.

During the period 1820-1821, Anna met and was attracted to the dashing, well-to-do Planter Captain and Colonel Adjutant H. C. Knudsen. Knudsen, at the time, was Chief Inspector of La Grande Princess, the model plantation owned by Count Schimmelman. This plantation was considered an outstanding one in St. Croix, not only because it was well run, but because of its humane and enlightened treatment of its workers, from slaves to management.

Evidently the attraction between Anna and Knudsen was a mutual one. It was not long before they were living together under one roof. Shortly thereafter, Knudsen purchased his own plantation, Belvedere, on the north side of the island. In 1824, Knudsen issued a public declaration to the effect that mahogany furniture purchased to furnish Belvedere belonged to Anna Heegaard. The furniture was listed: *two mahogany beds with five mattresses, two big mahogany eating tables, consisting of three simple tables, six mahogany tables, two sofas, 24 chairs, two big mirrors in mahogany frames, one mahogany sideboard, two mahogany chests of drawers.* Also included in the listing were *silverware, crockery, crystal glasses, table linen and kitchen utensils.*

At the time, Anna Heegaard owned fifteen slaves outright. Later she purchased a house, Compagnigade No. 5, in Christiansted, for the sum of 6250 Rigsdalers. From her girlhood, Anna had been impressed by her mother on the urgent need for security. Romance was one thing, stressed Susanna Uytendahl, but human relationships tended to end unexpectedly and abruptly at times. Heartaches were bad enough, but there was nothing worse than being left destitute.

Anna was smart enough to take care of herself, but mere accumulation of wealth was not enough to satisfy her sensitive spirit. Her nature rebelled against the social order that "trapped" her, and people like her, in a strange middle position between two worlds – black slaver and white population. Laws and regulations issued as far back as 1755 had guaranteed to the "free-coloured" equality with whites, but these laws and regulations had been sidetracked. To quote from the historian, Lawaetz:

"Authorities issued special statements all the time, restricting the rights of the 'free-coloured' population. These restrictions applied not only to the living but were to be Golden

Rules even for their children and grandchildren. Among the regulations was one that denied the 'free-coloured' citizenship, and through this, kept them out of certain offices and possibilities for work.

Free-coloured men could, if they were lucky, become fishermen, or learn certain small trades. The highest position a 'free-coloured' woman could reach was that of seamstress. Many of the men became vagabonds, and the women, prostitutes. This latter resort presented ample opportunities, because there were many soldiers and seamen in the islands.

Free-coloured women with good looks and good manners often associated with white civil servants, planters, merchants or sea captains. Men in these white groups were often unmarried or had left wives and children behind in Europe. They took these 'free-coloured' women into their homes as housekeepers, but everybody knew that they would live together as husbands and wives.

Some of these liaisons were short lived; some lasted longer. Often, one of the partners died, or the man might marry a white woman, or his legal wife might turn up. In many cases, however, these 'natural marriages' lasted for years. Paternity was established in each case. Children resulting from these 'natural unions,' were entered in Government Registers under the father's family name.

On the whole, being a 'free-coloured' was neither fish nor fowl. Since most of these 'free-coloured' were of an 'in-between' color, neither black nor white, their existence became very difficult, especially for the most reflective of them, or the very fair skinned."

Anna Heegaard's genealogical background was an interesting one. She was an "outside" descendant of one of the most prominent families of St. Croix. To quote from "Personal Historisk Tidsskrift," Danish Archives:

Anna Heegaard's mother was the 'free mulatto woman,' Susanna Uytendahl, born in St. Croix about 1774. Susanna was the illegitimate daughter of Charlotte Amalie Bernard, a slave woman, and Johannes Balthazar, eldest son of Lucas Uytendahl, Baron de Bretton.

Charlotte Amalie Bernard, (Anna's grandmother) was born in St. Croix, about 1753. She is supposed to be identical with the Negro woman, Amalie, or Charlotte Amalie, who appears in the Government Register several times. She was the property of Baron de Bretton.

Note: The Brettons were descendants of Huguenots, (French Protestants), who had come to the West Indies in the late 17th Century to escape religious persecution. Originally they had settled in St. Christopher, then in St. Thomas. Later, they moved to St. Croix.

According to archive material, the Brettons, on their mother's side, were descended from an old French noble family whose last representative was Admiral Jean Grace de Bretton. The Admiral, in turn was a direct descendant of another distinguished French Naval leader, Coligny. Admiral Jean Grave was related also to the families de Witt and Ruyter of Holland.

With this "fighting blood" in her veins, it is little wonder that Anna Heegaard was in the forefront of the battle to effect drastic reforms in the social system of the Danish West Indies.

In 1827, when Peter von Scholten came to St. Croix as Governor-General, he was entertained in great style. Gala events were held in his honor: sumptuous dinners, garden parties, balls. Planters attempted to outdo each other in trying to impress him and to gain his favor. Since Capt. Knudsen and his mistress, Anna Heegaard, attended many of these events for von Scholten, it was natural that their paths should cross. In fact, Anna made it her business to keep close to the Governor-General. In devious ways, she tried to attract his attention, to make him aware of her. She had long known of von Scholten's friendly and sympathetic attitude; of his many efforts to elevate the coloured people of the islands.

Once she had gotten close to him, Anna Heegaard let no opportunity go by to describe to von Scholten the plight of the "free-coloured;" the urgent need for reforms and the kind of reforms that were needed. She spoke to him of the humiliation the elite of her group felt in having to carry the so-called "freedomletter," a document that every "free-coloured" person had to carry to show that he or she was not a slave.

To quote, Lawaetz:

"These documents were offensive as they were all similar, without considering birth, culture or upbringing, their form giving the impression that the person only recently was freed, while his or her freedom might have originated from a great-grandmother. Some of the "free-coloured" were respected in the society, while some of the very recently freed, even dishonored the society. It was necessary to make distinct separations."

Indignation showed in Anna Heegaard's voice when she spoke to von Scholten about the widespread and officially sanctioned discriminatory employment; how talented and able people in her group were denied the right to work in any but the most menial jobs. She, and people like her, were deeply resentful of an official statement to the effect that if the "free-coloured" wanted jobs, there were plenty of such jobs in the cane fields with pay. "Never, never, said Anna Heegaard, would any 'free-coloured' person that she knew go back to the cane fields and join the toiling slaves for any kind of remuneration."

Von Scholten was impressed with the sincerity, dedication and intelligence of the young woman. Much of what she said to him touched deeply on problems in an area in which he had been trying to find workable solutions. Not only did this young woman know the problems intimately, but she had answers, and what she had to say made considerable sense.

It got to the point where von Scholten found himself seeking out Anna Heegaard to get her honest and intelligent opinions on just how he should cope with the many problems that daily arose between Planters and their slaves; "free-coloured" and a society that did everything but outrightly reject them.

This was the beginning of a relationship between Anna Heegaard and Peter von Scholten that was to deepen. They met often in his office, or at the nearby home of Councillor of Justice Gjellerup, an intimate friend of von Scholten, where the Governor-General often had his meals, and where he actually resided on occasions when Judge Gjellerup was absent from the island.

Von Scholten fell deeply in love with Anna Heegaard. She saw it coming and did nothing to stop it. It is recorded in "Personal Historisk Tidsskrift" that Anna Heegaard co-habited with von Scholten, early in the year 1828, in Gjellerup's house in Kongensgade in Christiansted.

For all his years of power and glory and accumulated honor, von Scholten was a human being, emotionally starved. The long separations from his wife had left him with pent-up feelings and desires that no amount of long hours and hard work could obliterate.

Note: Local Librarian and Archivist Enid Baa, in her intensive research, has come across a historic gem in von Scholten's personal life, which she has willingly shared with us:

In the baptismal records of the Catholic Church here, there is a record of a birth of a child, May 14, 1820. This child, a girl, Marie Marthe Peterette, was baptized on the 2nd of September, 1820. The father's name is listed as Peter Carl Frederick von Scholten; the mother's name, Marie Louise Josephine Deisgrotte. C.N.E. Stakemann is listed as Godfather; Francoise Touissine Arringner as Godmother.

When von Scholten became ill in the latter part of 1828, Anna visited him daily and did everything possible to nurse him back to good health. Capt. Knudsen, who was no fool, seemed to have been aware of the relationship that had developed between Anna and the Governor-General, but he did nothing to interfere with it. He knew that Anna was a headstrong, independent woman, and in light of von Scholten's serious illness and his pending departure from the island, Knudsen figured that the matter would "blow over" and that Anna would come back to where she "belonged."

When von Scholten left the islands on his trip northward, April 17, 1829, he carried with him a list of social conditions and desired reforms, prepared in conjunction with Anna Heegaard, to be shown to the Danish King. He carried with him, also, Anna's promise that when he returned, she would come to live with him and share his life.

When von Scholten arrived in Copenhagen he did not act like a man who had just recovered from a serious illness. He "bubbled" with the joy of living. His friends commented that he seemed "exhilarated," anxious to get his work done in the Danish capital and eager to return to the islands.

His family found him more jovial and generous than ever. Not only did he bring them valuable gifts from the islands, but during 1831, he insisted that the family move into better living quarters, a spacious and elegant house on Bredgade No. 186. (Nowadays No. 45).

There is a description of some of von Scholten's activities in Denmark during this period written by C. H. von Holten, a former Governor of St. Thomas, retired in Copenhagen. On the 27th January, 1832, shortly before von Scholten left for the islands, von Holten wrote home:.

"All the Princes, the Prime Ministers and the foreign Ambassadors were there, a couple of hundred persons. At midnight, two coloured trumpeters blew a fanfare, and von Scholten proposed a toast to his Majesty's birthday."

In an earlier entry in his diary, von Holten mentioned another incident, this time at a party, Dec. 26, 1831, at the luxurious quarters of the Danish Prince, Christian:.

"After a sumptuous banquet, the men retired to another room and began to gamble. Von Scholten lost 300 Dalers to Prince Ferdinand who was more used to losing than winning. The Prince was overjoyed and treated von Scholten like a long lost brother."

Von Holten was of the opinion that von Scholten had lost to Prince Ferdinand deliberately as part of his shrewd way of handling members of the Royal family.

As early as Jan. 9, 1830, Peter von Scholten made personal contact with the Danish King and told him that he, von Scholten, was deeply concerned with the problems of the "free-coloured" in the islands. He, von Scholten, knew the problems intimately and was convinced that he could offer solutions. What was most urgently needed were distinct regulations and clarification covering the basic rights of the "freecoloured." These regulations, to be truly effective, should come from the absolute King himself.

Beginning with a request that the so-called "freedom letter" be abolished, von Scholten listed in detail the von Scholten/Heegaard plan for social reform in the islands. The plan was approved, in its entirety by the Danish King, on April 10, 1830. Returning to the islands in the summer of 1832, von Scholten published the King's orders for social reform with these added comments:

"His Royal Majesty is convinced that the time has come to remove the erroneous opinions, the prejudice and the obstacles that have separated the two classes of citizens, and to promote the advance towards the "free-coloured." Those who have ears, listen! The King himself has spoken."

A Commission was appointed to study the new rules and regulations covering social justice and to begin to carry them out.

Anna Heegaard kept her promise. She moved in with von Scholten. For two to three years, they lived at William Newton's Plantation, the "Castle." In 1834, they moved to their own estate, *"Bülowsminde,"* outside Christiansted. At the time, von Scholten was 50 years of age, Anna Heegaard, 44.

H. C. Knudsen, the man who Anna Heegaard left for von Scholten, took the incident in his stride. Far from being emotionally wounded, he seemed friendly and philosophical about the whole affair. At a later date, he wrote to a friend in Denmark:

"I am very fond of von Scholten, and I am convinced that in his heart of hearts, he also likes me. But he never forgets, and cannot forget, that I am the one Anna Heegaard ever cared for and still cares for, strange as it may seem. Yet it is true."

"I firmly believe that von Scholten has never been so attached to, or cared so much for a woman, as he has for her. The bargain he made to secure her as his property was based upon very great promises."

SUSANNA UYTENDAHL (ANNA HEEGAARD'S MOM)
(1774–1847)

SUSANNA UYTENDAHL

Number	**B36**
Type	**Pictures**
Description	**Miniature painting by free mulatto Susanna Uytendahl (ca. 1774-1847), Kompagnigade 1, Christiansted, St. Croix.**
Remark	**Susanna Uytendahl (called "Mama Susanna") was born a house slave, but was bought free at the age of 12. Her father was from a plantation owner family and her mother was the house slave Charlotte Amalie Bernard (1753-1856). Susanna lived with three white men, in a so-called "natural marriage", and had a number of children with them. The eldest child was Anna Heegaard, who lived with Governor-General Peter von Scholten at Bülowsminde. Susanna was relatively wealthy and bought the still existing house, Kompagnigade 1 in Christiansted (on the corner of Kirkegade). Downstairs she had a knitting shop. - About her family relations, take a closer look at the pedigrees B4 and B6 and in lecture A98.** **Susanna Uytendahl is the great-great-great-great-grandmother of Jens Benoni Willumsen, No. Lightning.** **Susanna is used as the main character in a novel by the author Maria Helleberg: "Miss Suzanna, based on real events".** **Forlaget Forum, 2002, 174 pages.**
Period	**1800 - 1847**
Date note	**Unknown year**
Photographer	**Unknown**
Material	**color positive**

Clothes washing in the stream, St. Croix ca. 1844. Notice the woman at right in the background who has swollen legs because of elephantiasis. Colored drawing by Frederik von Scholten with the title "Bitling near West-End, Santa Cruz". Maritime Museum of Denmark, File No. 000034248.

CHAPTER XX

VARIOUS LETTERS OF INTEREST

THIS CHAPTER CONTAINS VARIOUS LETTERS OF INTEREST AS IT RELATES to the events of Emancipation, including letters from three doctors who treated Governor-General Peter von Scholten; letters from plantation owners, church officials, etc.

You will also find a letter of recommendation dated July 23, 1848, written by James A. Smith to Lewis Crooke, Esq. in favor of General Buddhoe which was supposed to accompany General Buddhoe to Tortola, British Virgin Islands.

Additionally, there's also various Proclamations by Danish officials as it related to disturbances the day of and shortly after Emancipation. It was Captain Irminger who had taken the authority upon himself to declare martial law.

During this tumultuous time, there were lots of ordinances, reports, declarations and new proclamations enacted to govern the newly-freed slaves in the Danish West Indies.

A Government Commission was also established in January of 1849 by Denmark to investigate the insurrection and its aftermath.

St. Croix - 23 July 1848

Dear friend,

Things have been with us from the night of the 2nd instant that it is past my ideas at present to describe, but the individual who will present this is the "Governor General John Gutlif Bordo," who took the island of St. Croix with an English flag at the head of his army. When I say "took the country," he demanded the Emancipation and no more. After he succeeded, he was perfectly satisfied, but his men in office was not satisfied to be free, but turned out right down robbers. They broke the courthouse as well as the Judge's Clarke house, destroyed his furniture. They then went aboard the Fort and attempted to enter. This happened on the 3rd day of July. One man, a great merchant Wlm. Moore who as well as all the white inhabitants took the Fort as his refuge, told them to fire on the negroes. The word was no sooner from his lips than they left the Fort and destroyed his well-furnished house and store, not leaving the carpet on the floor.

This man, General Burdo, who I recommend to your notice have been an honest and upright slave. He fought for freedom and as soon as he succeeded, he turned and subdued the people. He was guarded by our company and much thought and spoken of by the inhabitants of West End, for, through him, we have saved ourselves from shedding blood. My paper will not run much further it is all in haste.

He is a quiet man. In a strange land, he will feel quite odd. It is only for his safety that he is sent in your island for a short time. Our town might have been burnt to ashes was it not for him. He will be able to describe to you the particulars personally. Ask him where he went from estate-to-estate quailing [quelling] the people who were pilfering. He will tell you the whole matter, oh my friend.

On Tuesday the 4th instant there were about 3000 that came in town. Among them, about the half came with a bundle of cane trash and matches. What a horrible sight. But through this Burdo, they were quailed [quelled]. He was an acquaintance of mines whilst a slave. He now stands in promotion in this island as a honest and brave man! He is sent by a subscription. He have means. Should you see him the wrong way, for my sake, direct and forward him in the way which will promote him to respectability.

He have from our Major a letter to the authorities in Tortola, but they will not do the merciful. Any writing that he might require, you will greatly oblige me by doing it for him as though me. All his communications will be attended to.

My compliments to your family. I have also to acquaint you that on the 23rd morning of June, I was blessed with a second son. Thank God, mother and son are doing well, notwithstanding the wound. My best respects to Mrs. Crandle and the old man -- I meant Mother Lewis. Let me hear from you soon, at the same time let me know the situation of

General Burdo. This was intended as a copy, but unfortunately it is to be forwarded. In haste, I have forgotten to put my signature, to my epistle.

I am yours truly,

James A. Smith

Lewis Crooke, Esq.
Tortola.

Proven Copy filed - 22nd February 1849
C. Flensborg

~~~~#~~~~

Col de Nully

Dear Sir:

I beg leave to inform you that the negroes have kept up an alarm by ringing bells and blowing shells since 10 o'clock last night. Great excitement prevails from this westward. No alarm being made east of this. They collected in large numbers on the roads and used very bad language. They declare they will not work anymore. What is to be done in this dreadful state of things!

Upperlove 3 July 1848 5 a.m.
Your oft Servt
G.J. Mudie

~~~~#~~~~

At the request of General von Scholten, I beg leave to make the following statement concerning him:
I have, for many years been the medical adviser and attendant of General von Scholten and may therefore assert that I am well acquainted with the nature of his constitution as well as his usual disposition of mind and character.
In the morning of Thursday, the 6th of July 1848, I received an urgent message to come to the General quickly, as he was said to have become suddenly very ill. I found him in bed and, most evidently, under a smart hysterical attack. After a little while, he appeared somewhat calmer, and then complained of feeling weak, and of a confusion in the head and

an inability to concentrate his reasoning faculties on any particular subject, and repeatedly inquired of me if I thought he would go mad or would ever again be in his right senses.

He complained of no pain whatever in any part. He repeatedly put his hand on his head and said, *"I have lost this; I have lost this!"* He had no fever whatever. His corporeal health did not in any way seem to be impaired; but his mental agitation was so great that it rendered him perfectly incompetent to perform the duties of his office, especially during the state of insurrection and anarchy in which the negro agricultural population of the island then was and still is.

It was under these circumstances that Garrison Surgeon Knudsen and I gave a medical certificate on the strength of which a Government Commission was nominated by the General to act in his stead.

I have, of course, visited General von Scholten frequently since the 6th Instant. His corporeal health continued unimpaired. His mental condition, although in a much less agitated or disturbed state, still continues to such a degree as, in my opinion, to unfit him for the duties of his office as Governor-General. And, as I see no prospect of change in this respect, I thought it right to advise him to leave the island and repair to Europe.

That the preceding is, to the best of my knowledge and belief, a true statement of his case. I am willing, if required, to attest on oath.

Respectfully,

W.H. Ruan, M.D.

St. Croix, Christiansted

~~~~#~~~~

English Steamer *"Dee"*
Southampton 5th August 1848

Sir,

Having had the honor to attend Your Excellency in my professional capacity from the period when you embarked on board the *"Dee"* under circumstances calculated to command the respect and interest of all around you until arrival of the ship in England, an interval of these weeks, and having in consequence the best opportunity of knowing the state of health under which Your Excellency came on board at St. Thomas, and continued for some time subsequently, I feel it incumbent on me, on parting, to offer a few words of caution with reference to those symptoms of cerebral disturbances from which you suffered at the commencement of the voyage, and which indeed to greatly ameliorate had not yet entirely disappeared.

At the time when Your Excellency first did me the honor to consult me, I found you labouring under a high degree of nervous excitement accompanied by considerable physical depression, the result of excessive mental fatigue anxiety as well as of great bodily exhaustion.

In short, the symptoms presented to my observation were of character to indicate that serious disturbance of the nervous system had been produced by consistently harassing both to mind and body and operating for a length of time beyond that which nature could, with impunity, sustain without an adequate interval of repose.

It is my deliberate and decided opinion that had these causes continued to operate or had Your Excellency failed to adopt the necessary alternative of withdrawing at once and without delay from the climate of the West Indies, an attack of even a more grave character might probably have ensued and manifested itself either in the form of an apoplectic seizure or in some less sudden, but not less serious, evidence of organic mischief.

With these views impressed upon my mind, permit me in addition to such medical advice as I have already offered you, respectfully, but firmly, to represent to Your Excellency the importance of maintaining for a time the utmost mental tranquillity, and of avoiding as far as possible, for at least a brief period after your arrival, all sources of mental excitement. And that I am the more anxious to urge upon you from the belief that notwithstanding the very startling improvement in Your Excellency's health, precautionary measures are still essential to good perfect restoration.

In conclusion, allow me further to suggest that Your Excellency will do well to embrace the offer timely offered by your temporary sojourn in London, to consult your former medical attendant in England, Sir James Clarke, Physician to Her Majesty, who from his previous knowledge of Your Excellency's constitution and great experience in all matters connected with change of climate, would, I am satisfied, offer the most valuable opinion of which you can avail yourself.

Having occasion to write to Sir James, to whom I have the honor to be known, I will take care to mention to him the particulars of Your Excellency's case and that I have strongly recommended you to see him.

I beg leave to apologize for the length of this communication, and to remain, Sir, with the greatest respect.

> Your Excellency obedt humble servant
> Charles S. Webber, U.R.C.S.
> Surgeon *"Dee"*

Your Excellency General von Scholten
13th July 1848

~~~~#~~~~

We, the undersigned, do hereby solemnly declare and when required will be willing to attest on oath, that we are of the opinion that Governor-General von Scholten is in such a state of mind that he is unfit and unable to perform the duties of Governor-General, but that he is, notwithstanding, sufficiently collected in mind to appoint delegates to perform those duties.

Respectfully,

St. Croix,
Christiansted 7th July 1848   W. H. Ruan, MD   B. Knudsen

~~~~#~~~~

By request, I beg leave to state that in the course of many years of professional attendance on Counsellor Petersen and his family, I have had ample and numerous opportunities of observing the nature and peculiarities of his constitution. He is of a highly nervous temperament and when wrought upon by any particularly exciting cause, undergoes considerable mental agitation, as well as suffer from derangement of his corporeal functions. Such occurrences with him I have not unfrequently had occasion to witness.

The insurrection of the negro population of this island which occurred in July 1848, together with concomitant events, produced the above-mentioned effects in him to so great a degree that they entirely disqualified him, for a time, either from performing the duties of his office or any other important business.

In order to avoid the occurrence of a worse condition in him (which I then deemed very probable) I then thought it my duty to recommend for him a trip to Europe. From causes with which I am but imperfectly acquainted, this recommendation was not adopted.

I visited Counsellor Petersen yesterday and conversed with him for some time on various topics. I found him quite calm and collected in mind. His conversation was perfectly rational and indicated no mental aberration whatever. He is much emaciated and seem very much weakened in body. His countenance still bears on it an expression of anxiety and apprehension. And on my recommending to him gentle exercise in the open air by walking, that expression was changed to unease, aversion and dislike. And I was told by one of his friends present at the time, that they had not been able to persuade him to walk out.

From all of my observations during my visit, I certainly thought him very much recovered from his former state of health, both as to mind and body. But at the same time I am decidedly of opinion that any close attention to business or any unusual excitement would be extremely apt to bring on a relapse into his disorder, which might prove much more permanently injurious than his former attack.

From all these considerations, I am still led to the conclusion that a removal for some time from this island to other localities and scenes would prove amicably beneficial to him. I have therefore no hesitation in urgently recommending the adoption of such a measure.

That the preceding is my opinion of Counsellor Petersen's case. I am willing, if required, to attest on oath.

Christiansted 19th January 1849

~~~~#~~~~

Dear Sir:

Being informed that some trouble exists concerning the occurrences which took place in the Fort on the Monday of the insurrection I beg leave to inform you that it would afford me great pleasure in giving you further elucidations on the matter, if necessary.

I have no doubt they would contribute much to exculpate the Captain of the Fort from any blame which might have been attributed to him on that occasion. In justice to Captain Castonier, I can safely offer that he was one of the few officers who did not desert his post on that memorable day and showed great energy and judgment in the critical situation he was placed, especially when we take into consideration the small force at his command and the immense number of people, armed with every kind of dangerous weapons, he had to contend with.

It is my opinion, as well as the opinion of the gentlemen who were on the Battery on the said Monday, that if the people were fired upon the consequences would have been much worse.

To prevent these sad results, I came off the Battery twice on the parade ground at the expressed desire of some of the gentlemen there present to keep back the people from approaching the Fort and to dissuade the Captain from firing on them as there was no guarantee of the safety of the town or country.

Hoping you will excuse this trouble.

I remain, Sir, Yours Respectfully,
T.A. O'Ryan
Catholic Pastor

Frederiksted, March 1st, 1849

~~~~#~~~~

    We, the undersigned Planters and citizens of this jurisdiction have heard with regret and surprise that by a so-called commission in Christiansted your names have been excluded from among those named to direct affairs in this part of the country. To your talents and energy we are indebted for the preservation of our lives and we feel convinced that to the extent of your command, the town of Frederiksted has been saved from destruction by your exertions and to you chiefly we owe that the surrounding country has been brought to its present state of submission.

    We therefore assure you that as you possess our confidence we shall place no reliance upon any unauthorized arrangement by which you are excluded from the guidance of our affairs.

Frederiksted, St. Croix 8th July 1848

Respectfully,

John v. Brackle	James Codvice	H. Lowenson
Isaac Farrington	P. G. Heyliger	R. P. Hanson
R. T.Smith	J. Mudie	C. Doute
Wm Hardcastle	Robt Wm Tait	T. Spolton
E. Benjamin	Thomas Smith Barnes	David Finley
Wm Heyliger	E. Jones	J. Rasket
Foster Barnes	Thomas Armstrong	Thomas Rasket
John O'Connor	Joseph Smith	T. Mac Farlane
T. Sheridan	A. v. Brackle	Geo Henderson
T. A. O'Ryan (Cath Pastor)	Robert O'Terrale	H. Kierrumgaard
Wm Peebles	R.P. Worm	A. Hewson
P. Stafford	Wm Stedman	G.Bolton
J.A. Sundegaard	J. Quabe	James A. Clendinen
A. Cox	C. Beikehy	J. Morton
T. Huthington	T. Ross	J. Mac Pherson
Edward Hunter	Roger Terrale	

To: Kammerjunker & Capitain v. Castonier [Chamberlain & Captain Castonier] - Commander at the Fort at Frederiksted

[50 Signatures]

St. Thomas, Sammufere v. Oxholm

We, the undersigned Planters and citizens of the western jurisdiction of this island beg leave respectfully to apply to Your Excellency in our present dangerous and deplorable state of affairs.

In consequence of the want of all power in the authorities of sufficient military force, and according to our conviction of a constant system of tampering with the unfree population, we have seen our lives endangered in the most frightful manner and we see our properties destroyed and the earnings of many years of hard labor, which we hoped to enjoy under the protection of the Danish Government, sacrificed.

We feel that we owe our lives and whatever may be saved of our property to the energy and talents of the Captain of H.M. Brig *Ørnen,* and of Captain Castonier, the Commander of the Fort of Frederiksted, which town, but for them, would have been sacked and burnt.

Under these circumstances we have just heard that in consequence of the imminent dangerous state of health of the Governor-General v. Scholten and at the moment when he is said from a fit of apoplexy to be quite incapable of expressing his sentiments, a Commission has been appointed to administrate the island, the greater number of the members of which we have no confidence and we find that the Planters and respectable burghers of the island, whose interest are highly endangered and who, if this island is ever again to flourish as a Danish colony, must again reside among our now rebellious population, have been contemptuously thrown aside and their opinions and wishes and thoughts not thought worth consulting, while others have been preferred on whom we have no reliance.

We therefore beseech Your Excellency under our unhappy circumstances to come to our assistance by taking that station to which you are legally entitled by the commission you hold from His Majesty and thereby prevent the state of anarchy, which we otherwise fear may ensue.

Should the presence of Your Excellency by unavoidable circumstances be delayed, we humbly entreat you to appoint for this jurisdiction such an administration as we may have confidence in and we candidly confess that such cannot be the case with any from which the above-mentioned names are excluded.

St. Croix, the 7th July 1848.

~~~~#~~~~

PROCLAMATION

The country being in a disturbed state and, in consequence hereof declared under martial law, the commanders of the military forces are hereby empowered and ordered to search the whole of the country and take away, by any means, all arms found on the different estates and to take such positions and steps as at present may be found necessary for the purpose of controlling the whole of the country people.

Any person or persons opposing themselves to the orders of the officers in command will be shot on the spot, therefore the peaceable and well-disposed are ordered to separate themselves from the rioters if they will not share their fate.

Government House, St. Croix, 6th July 1848.

Kunzen	C.B. Petersen	Foester	Rothe
Friderichsen	H.L. Arnesen	Bahneberg	Carl Reimer

Pro vera copia [proven copy]
Flensborg, 12th January 1849

~~~~#~~~~

Lieut. Holstein:

Sir,

I beg leave to inform you that the Grove Place gang will not come out of their houses to hear the Proclamation read. They are not at work today.
Your obdt Serv

G. Jos Mudie
Grove Place
3 P.M. 28th September 1848

~~~~#~~~~

Her Majesty Ship *"Thunder"* at St. Thomas, 9th July 1848

Sir,

It being necessary that I should proceed as soon as possible in execution of other duties assigned to me, and from the continued peaceable state of the island, I have to beg Your

Excellence will be so good as to inform me whether you have reason to think that the presence of Her Majesty's Ship under my command in this port is any longer required for the preservation of lives and property.

I have the honor to be
Sir
Your most Obedient Servant

Edward Barnett
Captain

To His Excellence
Administering the Government
St. Thomas

~~~~#~~~~

St. Thomas, 9th July 1848

Sir,

In reply to your communication of this day, I have the satisfaction to say that I coincide with you in the opinion that the state of this island appears no longer to call for the presence of Her Majesty's Ship under your command, at the same time I beg you will accept of my best thanks for the service which you have rendered the island on the occasion and of which I shall not fail to make report to my government.

I have the honor to be
Sir
Your most obedient servant

H.H. Berg
Administering the Government

To:

Capitan Edward Barnett
Commanding H.B.M. Ship *"Thunder"*

~~~~#~~~~

It is hereby made known that after gunfire in the evening until daylight two or more individuals must not stand together in the streets or public places. Crowds gathering together at any time of the day will be dispersed by force.

The inhabitants are especially warned not to interfere with the Spanish soldiers. All arms in town not as yet delivered up are to be sent either to the Fort or to police offices without delay.

Frederiksted Police Office - October 29, 1848   C. Sarauw

~~~~#~~~~

May it please Your Excellency:

We the undersigned wardens and Vestry of St. Paul's Church, Frederiksted, respectfully take leave to inform Your Excellency that our Pastor, the Reverend William Allman, M.D., left the island on the 14th.

We therefore take the liberty to request your permission to allow the church to be open on Sundays and Holy-Days, and the service conducted by a member of the Vestry as heretofore during the absence of the officiating clergyman.

Respectfully,

R.T. Smith   Isaac Farrington
J. V. Heyliger   A. Straun
W. MacFarlane   J.A. Mudie

St. Croix – 7 August 1848

~~~~#~~~~

The extraordinary difficulties of the times must be our excuse for addressing Your Excellency with the following subject:

We are driven to the disagreeable necessity of requesting Your Excellency to make a change on the Commission established in Westend for the examination of prisoners.

Public confidence is everything at the present moment, and until that exist the peace of the country will not be restored. We find, though 8 culprits have been condemned and shot, and many others have undergone questioning, not one step, as far as we can learn, has been taken on the effort towards learning the plot formed among the negroes for liberating themselves in rebelling against Your Majesty's laws. And from the known sentiment of the first member of the Commission, Lieutenant Mothe, it is our opinion that he makes no effort to discover the real authors of the outbreak and various ramifications. And we fear that the motive or other evidence leading to such is thrown aside or quashed. Whether mistaken or not, in the opinion we have formed of Commander Mothe, we assure Your Excellency that to not profess the confidence of the public, who entertain the same opinion and feeling with regard to the second member of the Commission, namely Chamberlain Vice Stadthauptmand von Scholten, who during the late commotions has proved himself totally unworthy of that competency which ought to be placed in a man holding such responsible an office, and the members of the committee think it hard and unaccountable that their welfare should be sacrificed to the private views of these men.

We therefore beseech Your Excellency to remove them from the Commission. And if Your Excellency will allow the inhabitants of the island to choose of their number to be present at the meetings of the Commission in each jurisdiction, confidence will exist, the rumors will be put to a stop and we will be grateful to you for being the first supreme authority here showing an inclination to gratify the wishes of that part of the community certainly most interested in the welfare of the colony.

St. Croix - 25 July 1848

To: His Excellency
Chamberlain v. Oxholm Governor General

Respectfully,

Thomas Holbage	J. von Bretton	C. Lucas	David Finlay
William Woods	William von Bretto	J. Van Brackle	A. Newton
B. deNully	W. Bewitt	R. Knight	D.L. Finlay
J. de Pontavie	T.W. Armstong	J.G. Mudie	P. Hafford
Adam McCutchin	C. Johnson	John O'Reilly	J. Ruan
C. Kraus	J. van Berverhoudt	M. Newton	E. Jones
McCormick	G. Phillips	J. Plaskett	T. Murphy
Isaac Farringrton	P. McDermott	Frank Newton	R. Nesbitt
John Elliott	H. McEvoy	T. McEvoy	T. Rocke
J.Y. Stevens	J. Finlay	M. Scott	J. Abbott
Robert O'Ferrale	A. Balfour	J. Mudie	R. G. Knight
W. Hardcastle	R. F. Smith		

[46 SIGNATURES]

~~~~#~~~~

REPORT

Having received your Orders of the 11th to arrest the 33 negroes appointed by name and residence, I now have the honor to account to you for 31 of them. Martin King, I have not been able to trace.

With regard to Thomas at Spanish Town, I summoned that gang and Thomas would not come out and kept in his house. The driver and one of the gang sent by me for him, he rebelled against the driver, and ran away, perhaps wishing to give Thomas a chance to escape from the other which he attempted in vain.

Hearing a great noise in the yard, and leaving my horse charge, I took one of the troopers with me, and found Thomas in the house armed with a cudgel resisting the one man. The driver having run away as said, as Thomas refused my summons and attempted to resist, and even attacked me, I was under the necessity to fire at him, which proved mortal.

The driver of Spanish Town said that Thomas had a saber wound on his head, having in company with six others attacked Mr. Dardis and Mr. Helberg on the night of the 6th between Barren Spot and Spanish Town, which was presumed to be the reason why he would not allow himself to be captured.

St. Croix, 13th July 1848.

Your obt Servant
H. Elliott
act. LM: K.L.E.

To:
Colonel de Nully

~~~~#~~~~

May it please Your Excellency:

We, the undersigned inhabitants of this island learned with feelings of deep regret that in consequence of ill health Your Excellency has been induced to resign the command of the islands and is obliged to seek in Europe the establishment of Your Excellency's health, we avail ourselves of this opportunity to confess to Your Excellency our sentiments of high esteem and deep devotion.

During a number of years that Your Excellency has been entrusted with the command of these islands, we feel happy in the reminiscence that Your Excellency has invariably made it your chief study to promote the welfare of all His Majesty's subjects. Your Excellency has long possessed the cordial esteem of the good and liberal minded -- the friends of progression.

We cannot but regret the late excesses in our sister colony of St. Croix which no human being could have foresaw or anticipated under the mild and beneficent rule of Your Excellency. We are in this exigency unavoidably deprived of Your Excellency's long experience and great judgment.

We trust the Almighty disposer of all events will soon restore Your Excellency to health so that Your Excellency may be enabled to assume once more your high position among us and continue in the satisfactory performance of your duties to obtain the good will and approbation of all.

We are with sentiments of the highest consideration.

Your Excellency's
Most devoted & obedient servants

[Followed by 53 signatures]

St. Thomas the 15th of July 1848

| Peter James | Santorious Wright | Jos. Wotterding |
| Carl Wilhelm | H.Y. Stubbs | Uttehndahl Friborg |

To:
His Excellency
Major General, Chamberlain P. von Scholten
Grand Cross of the Order of Dannebrog and Dannebrogmand
Governor General of the Danish West Indian Islands

~~~~#~~~~

His Excellency
Chamberlain v. Oxholm, K.D. Governor-General

With reference to the interview which I had the honor to have with Your Excellency in Government House on Monday the 31st ult., and especially in reference to what then happened in respect to the application which I had been requested to make to N.V. McDermott, the Attorney and Manager of the Estate Rattan, namely that three young people on that estate might return to their parents living on the Estate Cane Valley, I beg leave, most respectfully, to submit the following statement:

In the Year 1843, the Estate St. Georges Hill was dismantled and the greater number of the negroes were removed, partly to the Estate Cane, situated in the immediate neighborhood of St. Georges Hill, and partly to the Estate Rattan, situated in the jurisdiction of Christiansted and at a distance of several miles from St. Georges Hill.

The house servants and their children were permitted to remain in the service of their former owner, N.V. Robe. But at his death, in July 1845, the removal of these servants took place.

Among these house servants was the woman Madelaine, wife of the head stock keeper on the adjoining Estate Cane Valley. This woman who had always been industrious and had saved some money was enabled to obtain her freedom. Her three eldest children (Abram, Joseph & Margaret (alias Sue) was removed to the Estate Rattan, and the mother with two youngest children passed her abode at Cane Valley. It having been agreed upon between M. Tower and myself that the two children were to be maintained by me until they attained that age when they could be legally separated from their mother.

I may state here that the parents informed me that M.V. Tower promised that the boy Abram, who was house servant with N.V. Robe, should be put to a trade. He was accordingly placed with the masons and received tools from M.V. Tower. But immediately after M.V. Tower's departure from the island the promise was broken and the boy was sent to the field.

Although the distance from Cane Valley to Rattan is so great, the mother has walked there almost every Saturday (thereby losing a day of her own labor) to see her children and to carry them their washed and mended clothes.

The parents now wish for the return of their children, not only that they may have them under their own care and protection, but that by uniting the labor of all, the whole family might live in a better and more comfortable manner. The young people also wish to return to their parents.

In opposition to this request, NV McDermott has appealed to Your Excellency, but I rely with the most perfect confidence that Your Excellency will view this case as one deserving your most favorable consideration, and that Your Excellency's high authority will be interposed that the reasonable request of the parents and children may be complied with.

Most respectfully,
J.Y.W. Caul
Cane Valley - August 7, 1848

~~~~#~~~~

NEIGHBORS AFTER EMANCIPATION

EPILOGUE

JOHN "GENERAL BUDDHOE" GOTTLIEB took that great and mighty walk of humanity when on Monday, July 3, 1848, he dared to stand up and lead the most brilliantly executed fight for freedom in the Caribbean, and mind you, without bloodshed. Remember, not a single white inhabitant of this island was killed or wounded, while General Buddhoe did his best to prevent bloodshed on the plantations. Unfortunately, those killed were the slaves judged to be found guilty and executed for their "so called offences" during the emancipation events (a total of 17 were executed by the authorities). Additionally, those summarily executed in Christiansted's two-day massacre only demonstrated the great fear and cowardice of some of the Danish officials involved. Later reports plantation-by-plantation would reveal just a few killed or wounded on each plantation, while the majority of plantations reported "none" dead or wounded.

General Buddhoe dared to walk on the stage of human history in a very admirable, courageous and distinctive way. Evidence shows that he collaborated and used his friendship with the Governor-General and other Danish authorities to strategically secure the Emancipation for his people. He did not allow this friendship to ultimately not be of great benefit to his fellowmen. This display of character and intellect, while facing impending execution, speaks to the man, his strong mind and aptitude. General Buddhoe was a master strategist and employed his strategy with perfect unwavering precision. Many neighboring Caribbean islands' fight for freedom (including our very own, St. John 1733 Revolution) was extremely bloody. St. Croix managed to have a bloodless revolution. This is extremely commendable!

The aftermath of the Emancipation saw General Buddhoe calming and controlling the furious, angry and, in some cases justifiably so, vengeful slaves, specifically on every north side, western and southern plantation. The same was done by **ADMIRAL MARTIN KING** from his very own Bog of Allen to Mount Pleasant, Slob, Glynn, Mon Bijou, Kingshill, Strawberry, Diamond & Ruby, all the estates in between and even as far east as Christiansted, where King had personally witnessed the entrails of some of his comrades oozing out of their bodies while they lay dead in the streets of Christiansted. Though he at first wanted blood-for-blood and life-for-life, he later wholeheartedly embraced peace and quickly exercised his influence over his comrades to calm the masses. This too painted a picture of his determination and resilience in the face of tumultuous circumstances. Martin King was honest. He quickly became a wanted man. Consequently, he escaped to the hills for a few days, but then would later turn himself in.

Interestingly, General Buddhoe and Admiral Martin King had never met prior to Emancipation and did not know each other, but like clockwork, they proceeded to respond in a similar manner the days following the Emancipation by quelling any and all potentially destructive behaviors on the various plantations where they both exhibited great influence and leadership.

We can surmise that etched deeply in the consciousness of both General Buddhoe and Admiral Martin King was the indisputable knowledge that slavery had already tampered with nature and had created way too many unspeakable incurable maladies. Their high level of consciousness allowed them to make the right choice of not further tampering with and/or creating or contributing to any more pain or sorrow among the newly freed slaves. For this very reason, I referred to both men as **"HONORABLE."**

The aspirations of our ancestors became a reality. All they wanted was their freedom…. their immediate emancipation…. and they were determined not to have to wait 12 years, as decreed, to obtain it. So they took it! The slave population found themselves united in their collective silence and in their collective action. They were also willing to risk their very lives for their freedom. The ultimatum was given. Many women, including two "Janes" (Jane Petersen and Jane Buntin, both of Plantation Prosperity) had already organized the women on the plantations, gathered the cane trash (bagasse) and came to town early ready to burn, if that became necessary.

Credit must also be given to Major Jacob Gyllich, who included both General Buddhoe and Admiral Martin King in his entourage as he traversed from plantation to plantation with other Danish officials to read the Proclamation. Honorable mention also of Lieutenants Richard Beech and Robert J. Robinson (both of the Brand Corps) who were part of that entourage.

Undoubtedly, General Buddhoe went to his grave with his secret, though he faced torture and ill treatment during his 25 days aboard the *Ørnen* and was questioned by Captain Irminger daily in the cabin up until Monday, January 8, 1849. He, nonetheless, remained silent. Governor-General Peter von Scholten on the other hand, confessed his secret of collaboration between the two men to his childhood friend and did not take the secret to his grave.

Raw unaltered information from the Danish archives depositions and court trials may have come close to aptly describe (in each testifiers' own words) the dynamics of this period of our proud history, but still the experience must have been both overwhelming and heavy-laden with much tears, joy and even wonderment not knowing what emancipation would truly bring.

Let us all take **A CLOSER LOOK** at our ancestors' rise out of the darkness of slavery in the Danish West Indies to the light of emancipation from chattel enslavement. As we are obligated to honor their memories, let us also commit ourselves, individually and collectively, to honor their enormous sacrifices and legacy by letting their truth be told…. one chapter at a time.

Thank you for your interest in this amazing work!!!

~~~~KATHLEEN~~~~

REFERENCES

DANISH-TO-ENGLISH TRANSLATIONS

Niklas Thode Jensen, Archivist
Senior Researcher, PhD.
Colonial History - Danish West Indies and India 1700s and 1800s
Danish National Archives. Arkivalieronline - Rigsakivet State Archives
(Original Contact and Referral)

~~~~~

BC Oversaettelse og archivhjaelp
BC Translation and Archive Service
Birgit Christensen, PhD., mag. art.
Billesborgvej 6 A
DK 2720 Vanlose, Denmark

(Translations done by: Birgit Christensen, PhD)

The West Indian Government, The Military Court in Frederiks Fort, Protocol of Justice Vestindiske Regering, Den Militære Standret i Frederiks Fort Justitsprotokol, Danish National Archives. Arkivalieronline - Rigsakivet State Archives

Chamber of Customs and Commerce Colonial and Trade Office.
On the Commission Appointed to Investigate the West Indian Government Officials' Conditions on the Emancipation in 1848 and the Trial of Governor-General Peter von Scholten, Danish National Archives. Arkivalieronline - Rigsakivet State Archives

Government-General Files Relating to Register of Correspondence Series B Police, Jails and Prison Matters, Danish National Archives. Arkivalieronline - Rigsakivet State Archives

~~~~~

Karen V. Sivertsen, PhD.
Aarhus University
School of Culture and Society
Department of Archaeology and Heritage Studies
Aarhus, Denmark

(Translations done by: Karen V. Sivertsen, PhD)

Danish Text to English Translations:
Pages 83, 87, 88, 97 and 105-107

BOOKS AND PUBLICATIONS

Beckles, Hilary Dr. – *Caribbean Slave Society and Economy*, AbeBooks - 1991

Hall, Neville A.T. – *Slave Society in the Danish West Indies*, University of the West Indies Press - April 1992

Hansen, Thorkild -- *Islands of Slaves*, English Edition, Sub-Saharan Publishers - 2005

Knox, John P. – *A Historical Account of St. Thomas, W.I.*, C. Scribner - 1852

Lewisohn, Florence – *St. Croix under Seven Flags*, The Dukane Press - 1970

Paiewonsky, Isidor -- "History Corner" *Anna Heegaard, Mistress of Governor General Peter von Scholten*, Virgin Islands Daily News, Published 1976

Petersen, Bernhard von – *A Brief Account About the Danish West Indian Islands – St. Croix, St. Thomas and St. Jan, Kjöbenhavn* - 1855

Taylor, Charles – *Leaflets from the Danish West Indies*, Praeger - 1888

Vraa, Mich – *Peter's Kraerlighed*, Lindhardt og Ringhof - 2017

NARRATIVES AND REPORTS

Narrative of the Insurrection of 1848 by Frederik von Scholten – Courtesy Whim Museum

Narrative of the Insurrection of 1848 by Captain Carl Irminger – Courtesy Whim Museum

Historic Furnishings Report
Fort Christiansvaern National Historic Site – 1988 – Courtesy National Park Service

Peter von Scholten's Letter to His Attorney Liebenberg – December 22, 1849

Peter von Scholtens forklaring pa oproret i 1848 og ophrevelsen af slaveriet (1849) – Courtesy Whim Museum

HISTORICAL RECORDS

Rigsakivet State Archives, Vibrog Denmark

Arkivalieronline – Danish National Archives

Family Search Historical Records

Frederiksted Birth Records – 1750-1850

Danish West Indies Censuses (1846-1860)

Prison Censuses – 1840-1841 and 1848-1855

Record of Deaths – English Church (Christiansted), July 1848

Burial Records (Frederiksted and Christiansted)

Frederiksted Baptism, Confirmation Records (Various Churches)

Plantation-by-Plantation Reports

OTHER SOURCES

Emancipation Commemoration Booklets (1948, 1973 and 1998)

St. Croix Avis Newspaper – 1848

St. Thomas Tidende Newspaper – 1848

GRAPHICS, IMAGES AND ILLUSTRATIONS

Front and Back Cover Graphic Design - Kathleen D. Dowling and Michael White

Hogensborg Plantation *(Page 8)* - Courtesy of Alamy

Frederik von Castonier Image *(Page 9)* - Royal Danish Library

Frederiks Fort With Whipping Post *(Page 14)* - Courtesy of Alamy

Anton von Falbe Grave Site Image *(Page 18)* - Danish Cemetery, Christiansted

Gendarmerie Barracks *(Page 24)* - Courtesy of PICRYL D.W.I. Images

Interior Frederiks Fort *(Page 26)* - 1760 - Courtesy of Trip Bucket

St. Croix Map (With Designated 9 Quarters) *(Page 37)* - Living on St. Croix.com

Frederik von Scholten Image *(Page 39)* - Courtesy of Wikipedia

Frederik von Scholten Grave Site Image *(Page 48)* - Dkconsulateusvi.com

Plantation La Grange – 1838 *(Page 49)* - St. Thomas Source

Carl Ludvig Irminger *(Page 50)* - Courtesy of Wikipedia

Interior Fort Christiansvaern *(Page 60)* - National Park Service Report

Printed Emancipation Proclamation *(Page 61)* - JSTOR

John "General Buddhoe" Gottlieb Image *(Page 63)* - St. Thomas Source

General Buddhoe's Baptismal Certificate *(Page 64)* - Frederiksted Lutheran Church Records

General Buddhoe's Family Information *(Pages 65-71)* - Danish West Indies Census Records

Leah "Sanchy" Petrus Police Report *(Page 72)* - Arkivalieronline

Admiral Martin King Photograph *(Page 74)* - 150th Emancipation Commemoration Booklet

Admiral Martin King's Family Information *(Pages 75-82)* - FamilySearch.org Historical

General Buddhoe's Fort Christiansvaern Image *(Page 85)* - 150th Emancipation Booklet

R.H. Amphlett Leader "Mensis Mirabilis" *(Page 86)* - Centennial Emancipation Booklet

Sugar Mill at Plantation Rust-Op-Twist *(Page 93)* - Courtesy of Wikipedia

Bookkeeper's Record of Buddhoe's C'sted Imprisonment *(Page 95)* - Arkivalieronline

Public Well at Watergut, Christiansted *(Page 102)* - PICASA

Bookkeeper's Record of Reward for Martin King *(Page 104)* - Arkivalieronline

Buddhoe's 1846 Census Report *(Page 109)* - Arkivalieronline

Buddhoe's Police Records of Arrest *(Pages 110-111)* - Arkivalieronline

Vague Listing of Wounded and Dead *(Page 113)* - Arkivalieronline

Book Excerpt *(Page 114)* - *"Islands of Slaves"* (Thorkild Hansen)

Christiansted Historic Site with All Six Buildings *(Page 124)* - National Park Service

Image Fort Commander Anton Falbe *(Page 125)* - Fort Christiansvaern Historic Report

Image Carl Ludwig Gjellerup *(Page 126)* - Fort Christiansvaern Historic Report

1850 Census *(Page 128)* - Arkivalieronline

Major Gyllich Grave Stone *(Page 129)* - DK Consulate (Holy Trinity Lutheran Church)

Frederiks Fort Floor Plan 1780 *(Page 130)* - National Park Service Report, Atlanta

Frederiks Fort Photographs *(Pages 132-133)* - National Park Service, Atlanta

Christiansvaern Fort Powder Magazine Room *(Page 133)* - National Park Service, St. Croix

Book Excerpt *(Page 134)* - *"Islands of Slaves"* (Thorkild Hansen)

Record of Deaths *(Pages 143-146)* - English Church Christiansted

Captain Carl Ludvig Christian Irminger Image *(Page 148)* - Courtesy of Wikipedia

Four Screenshot Images *(Page 149-151)* - Courtesy of Wikipedia

His Majesty's Brig of War *Ørnen* *(Pages 153-154)* - Courtesy of Wikipedia

Shipping Records *(Page 155)* - St. Thomas *Tidende* Newspaper - 1848

Governor-General Peter von Scholten Image *(Page 159)* - Courtesy of Wikipedia

Mich Vraa Book Cover *(Page 160)* - Google Search

Annaly Bay Tide Pools *(Page 166)* - Courtesy of Afar

Sugarcane Field Laborers *(Page 166)* - Library of Congress Jack Delano Collection

Prince Valdemar of Denmark Visits St. Croix 1879 *(Page 171)* - Courtesy

Ruins Mount Victory School *(Page 178)* - St. Croix USVI Travel Guide

Anna Elizabeth Ulricka Heegaard Image *(Page 180)* - Genealogy.com

Cartouche Map of Enslaved Children *(Page 183)* - Danish Archives Chamber of Revenue

Inventory of Heegaard's Slaves *(Page 185)* - Arkivalieronline

Bülowsminde Image *(Page 187)* - Islands of Slaves (Thorkild Hansen)

Anna Heegaard's Grave Stone Image *(Page 188)* - Courtesy Whim Museum

Susanna Uytendahl Image *(Page 196)* - ArchvDK

Clothes Washing Drawing by Frederik von Scholten *(Page 198)* - JSTOR

Neighbors After Emancipation Image *(Page 215)* - St. John Source

Bust of General Buddhoe *(Page 227)* - Buddhoe Park, Frederiksted

TACTICAL GENIUS AND MASTER STRATEGIST

ABOUT THE AUTHOR

NOTA BENE

Born in the beautiful town of Frederiksted on St. Croix, Virgin Islands, Kathleen D. Dowling, spent 33 years (1984-2017) in her professional career as a Court Reporter/Stenographer, first at the District Court of the Virgin Islands (1987-1990) and later during the 19th–32nd Legislatures of the Virgin (1991-2017), from where she is now retired. Dowling was named Employee of the Month (2003) and Employee of the Year (2013).

While on the job, she was noted for always highlighting and celebrating both Black and Virgin Islands History Months and is the author of a publication booklet *called "Little Known Facts of our Virgin Islands Heroes,"* which she self-published yearly in multiple editions, featuring various themes such as *"Names on our Schools," "Names on our Housing Communities," "Our Sports Heroes"* and many others. These publications were read over the inter-island intercom system of the Legislature every morning by employees and students.

She was also known for having yearly historically-based displays on the grounds of the Virgin Islands Legislature, including one called *"The Virgin Islands March In Living Color,"* where, using artifacts, figurines, coral sand and pictures, she literally depicted the lyrics of the *Virgin Islands March* in real-time. This creatively-brilliant display made the front page of the St. Croix Avis in 2016. Dowling knows that having your name on a product tends to make you take a closer look before it goes out the door, and she once told a colleague, *"words are what we do best….listening, writing, proofreading and producing verbatim transcripts, so let us always be consistent with accuracy, professionalism and quality."*

Based on extensive research, **A Closer Look at Emancipation 1848** makes a truly original contribution to understanding our celebrated Emancipation of July 3, 1848.

Milton Keynes UK
Ingram Content Group UK Ltd.
UKHW051948280524
443210UK00005B/42